- *The Beatitudes* -

A MAN WHO PURSUES TRUE BLESSING

DR. JAEROCK LEE

> "Blessed is the man who trusts in the LORD
> and whose trust is the LORD.
> For he will be like a tree planted by the water,
> that extends its roots by a stream
> and will not fear when the heat comes;
> but its leaves will be green,
> and it will not be anxious in a year of drought
> nor cease to yield fruit."
>
> *(Jeremiah 17:7-8)*

A MAN WHO PURSUES TRUE BLESSING by Dr. Jaerock Lee

Published by Urim Books (Representative: Kyungtae Noh)
73, Yeouidaebang-ro 22-gil, Dongjak-Gu, Seoul, Korea
www.urimbooks.com

All rights reserved. This book or parts thereof may not be reproduced in any form, stored in a retrieval system, or transmitted in any form or by any means, electronic, mechanical, photocopying, recording or otherwise, without prior written permission of the publisher.

Unless otherwise noted, all Scripture quotations are taken from the Holy Bible, NEW AMERICAN STANDARD BIBLE, ®, Copyright © 1960, 1962, 1963, 1968, 1971, 1972, 1973, 1975, 1977, 1995 by The Lockman Foundation. Used by permission.

Copyright © 2009 by Dr. Jaerock Lee
ISBN: 978-89-7557-215-9, ISBN: 978-89-7557-060-5(set)
Translated by Dr. Esther K. Chung. Used by permission.

Previously published in Korean by Urim Books, Seoul, Korea.
Copyright © 2007 by Dr. Jaerock Lee

First Edition May 2009
Second Edition August 2009

Edited by Dr. Geumsun Vin
Designed by Editorial Bureau of Urim Books
Printed by Yewon Printing Company
For more information contact at urimbook@hotmail.com

A Message on Publication

There is a story written in a university in Rome. A college student who had some financial difficulties went to a rich old man to ask for help. The old man asked him where he would spend the money. The student replied it was to finish his studies.

"And then?"

"I have to earn money."

"And then?"

"I will get married."

"And then?"

"I will get old."

"And then?"

"I will finally die."

"And then?"

"…"

There is a good lesson in this story. If the student were a person who was seeking true blessings that he could possess forever, he would have answered, "I will go to heaven," to the old man's last question.

Generally, in this society people think having things like wealth, health, fame, authority, and peace in family are blessings. They strive to have these things. But if we look around, we can find that there are few who enjoy all these blessings.

Some families may be rich, but many of them have problems or trouble in the relations between the parents, children, or in-laws.

Even a healthy man may lose his life at any moment due to accident or disease.

In April 1912, thousands of people were peacefully traveling on a luxurious cruise ship that had a tragic accident. The 'Titanic,' with 2,300 people onboard, collided with an iceberg and sank on her first cruise. It was the biggest cruise ship in the world boasting of its excellence and luxury, but nobody knew what would happen in just a few hours.

Nobody can tell about tomorrow for sure. Even if one may enjoy wealth, fame, and authority in this world for his whole life, he cannot be a blessed man if he falls into hell and suffers forever. Therefore, the true blessing is to receive salvation and enter into the kingdom of heaven.

About 2,000 years ago, Jesus began His public ministry with the message, "Repent, for the kingdom of God is near!" The first message that followed this proclamation was the 'Beatitudes,' with which they could reach the kingdom of heaven. To the people who would soon disappear like fog, Jesus taught about the eternal blessing, namely the true blessings to go into the kingdom of heaven.

He also taught them to become the light and salt of the world, to fulfill the Law with love, and to accomplish the Beatitudes. This is written from Matthew chapter 5 to chapter 7. This is called the 'Sermon on the Mount.'

Expressly, together with the Spiritual Love in 1 Corinthians chapter 13 and the Fruit of the Spirit in Galatians chapter 5, the Beatitudes tell us the way to become a man of spirit.

They are a signpost for us to be able to check ourselves, and the essential contents for us to become sanctified and enter into New Jerusalem which houses the throne of God and which is the most glorious dwelling place in heaven.

This book *A Man Who Pursues True Blessing* is a summary of the sermons about the Beatitudes that I delivered in the church a couple of times.

If we accomplish the words in the Beatitudes, we will not only enjoy all the blessings of this world such as wealth, health, fame, authority, and peace in the family, but we will also possess New Jerusalem among many heavenly dwelling places. The blessing given by God cannot be shaken in any kind of difficulties. If we only accomplish the Beatitudes, we won't have any deficiencies.

I pray that, through this book, many people will change into men of spirit who seek true blessings and receive all the blessings prepared by God. I also give thanks to Geumsun Vin, Director of Editorial Bureau, Manmin Central Church and the workers.

Jaerock Lee

Table of Contents

A Message on Publication

Chapter 1 : The First Blessing

Blessed Are the Poor in Spirit,
for Theirs Is the Kingdom of Heaven   1

Chapter 2 : The Second Blessing

Blessed Are Those Who Mourn,
for They Shall Be Comforted   21

Chapter 3 : The Third Blessing

Blessed Are the Gentle,
for They Shall Inherit the Earth   37

Chapter 4 : The Fourth Blessing

Blessed Are Those Who Hunger
and Thirst for Righteousness,
for They Shall Be Satisfied   55

Chapter 5 : The Fifth Blessing

**Blessed Are the Merciful,
for They Shall Receive Mercy**   69

Chapter 6 : The Sixth Blessing

**Blessed Are the Pure in Heart,
for They Shall See God**   89

Chapter 7 : The Seventh Blessing

**Blessed Are the Peacemakers,
for They Shall Be Called Sons of God**   105

Chapter 8 : The Eighth Blessing

**Blessed Are Those Who Have Been Persecuted
for the Sake of Righteousness,
for Theirs Is the Kingdom of Heaven**   125

Chapter 1
The First Blessing

Blessed Are the Poor in Spirit, for Theirs Is the Kingdom of Heaven

Matthew 5:3

*Blessed are the poor in spirit,
for theirs is the kingdom of heaven.*

A convict sentenced to death in an American prison was shedding tears as he held a newspaper in his hand. The headline was about the inauguration of the twenty-second president of the United States of America, Stephen Grover Cleveland. A jailer who was watching him asked him why he was crying so bitterly. He began to explain with his head down.

He continued saying, "Stephen and I are from the same college. One day, after we had finished our class, we heard the sound of a church bell. Stephen urged me to come with him to the church, but I refused. He headed to the church, and I to a pub. That made our lives so different."

A moment's choice changed the whole life of this man. But, this is not just about life on this earth. Our eternal life can also be changed because of the choices we make.

Those Invited to Heavenly Banquet

In Luke chapter 14, one man gave a big dinner banquet and invited many people. He sent his servants to escort the invitees, but all of the servants came back alone. The invitees had many reasons, but they were all too busy to come.

"I have bought a piece of land and I need to go out and look at it. Thank you for the invitation, but regretfully, I cannot come."

"I have bought five yoke of oxen, and I am going to try

them out. I am so sorry but I will not be able to attend."

"I know you will understand that I recently took a wife in marriage and for that reason I cannot come."

The host of the dinner sent his servants again to the village to bring the poor, the blind, and the lame from the streets to share in the banquet. In this parable Jesus compares those who received the invitations to those who have been offered an invitation to attend a heavenly banquet.

Today, those who are rich in spirit refuse to accept the gospel. They give many excuses for not attending while those who are poor in spirit quickly accept the invitation. That is why the first gate to pass through to true blessing is to become a person who is poor in spirit.

The Poor in Spirit

To be "poor in spirit" is to have a poor heart. It is having a heart that has no arrogance, pride, selfishness, personal desires, or evil. Thus, those who are "poor in spirit" accept the gospel easily. After accepting Jesus Christ, they long for spiritual things. They are also able to change quickly by the power of God.

Some women say, "My husband is a really good man, but he does not want to accept the gospel." People consider somebody to be "good" if he does not outwardly commit acts that are evil. But even though one seems to be good, if he does not accept the gospel because his heart is rich, how can we say he is really good?

In Matthew chapter 19, one young man came to Jesus and asked what good things he had to do to gain eternal life. Jesus told him to keep all the commandments of God. Then in addition to that, He told him to sell all his possessions, give to the poor, and then to follow Him.

The young man thought he loved God and kept His commandments very well. But he went away grieving. It's because he was rich, and he considered his wealth more precious than gaining eternal life. Seeing him Jesus said, *"It is easier for a camel to go through the eye of a needle, than for a rich man to enter the kingdom of God"* (v. 24).

Here, being rich does not just mean having possessions and great wealth. It means to be rich in spirit. People who are rich in spirit may not do something very evil on the outside, but have strong fleshly worldly desires. They take delight in money, authority, knowledge, pride, recreational activities, entertainment, and other pleasures. That is why they don't feel the need for the gospel, and they don't seek God.

Blessing of Richness for those who Are Poor in Spirit

In Luke chapter 16, the rich man enjoyed himself and gave

parties everyday. He was so rich that his heart was also rich; he didn't feel the need to believe in God. But the beggar Lazarus was suffering from diseases and had to beg at the gate of the rich man's house. Because he was poor in spirit, he sought God.

What was the result after they died? Lazarus was saved and could rest at the bosom of Abraham, but the rich man fell to the Hades and came to suffer forever.

The flames were so hot that he said, *"Father Abraham, have mercy on me, and send Lazarus so that he may dip the tip of his finger in water and cool off my tongue."* He couldn't get away from the pain even for a moment (v. 24).

Then, what kind of person is a blessed man? It is not the man who has so much possessions and authority and enjoys his life on this earth like the rich man. Though his life is lowly, it is a truly blessed life to accept Jesus Christ and enter into heavenly kingdom like Lazarus. How can we compare life on this earth, which is only for seventy or eighty years, with the eternal life?

This parable tells us that the important thing is not whether or not we are rich on this earth, but to be poor in spirit and to believe in God.

It does not mean, however, a person who has a poor spirit and has accepted Jesus Christ has to live a poor life and suffer from diseases like Lazarus, to be saved. But rather, because Jesus redeemed us from our sins and lived a life in poverty Himself, when we are poor in spirit and live by the word of God, we can be rich (2 Corinthians 8:9).

3 John 1:2 says, *"Beloved, I pray that in all respects you may prosper and be in good health, just as your soul prospers."* As our soul prospers, we will be healthy spiritually and physically, and we will receive blessings of finance, peace of family, and so on.

Even though we have accepted Jesus Christ and come to enjoy the blessing of richness, we have to keep our faith in Christ until the end to possess the heavenly kingdom completely. If we get away from the way of salvation by loving this world, our names can be erased from the book of life (Psalm 69:28).

This is just like a marathon race. When the marathoner who is running first goes away from the course before the finish line, he cannot get any prize not to mention the gold medal.

Namely, even if we are leading a diligent Christian life right now, if we become rich in heart again due to the temptations of money and worldly pleasures, our fervor will cool down. We may even depart from God. If we do, then we will not be able to reach the kingdom of heaven.

That is why 1 John 2:15-16 says, *"Do not love the world nor the things in the world. If anyone loves the world, the love of the Father is not in him. For all that is in the world, the lust of the flesh and the lust of the eyes and the boastful pride of life, is not from the Father, but is from the world."*

Cast off the Lust of the Flesh

The lust of the flesh is the thoughts of untruth that arise in the heart. These are the natures that want to commit sins. If we have hatred, anger, desires, envy, an adulterous mind and arrogance in our heart, we will want to see, hear, think, and act following these natures.

For example, if a person has the nature to judge and condemn others, they will have the desire to hear rumors about others. Then, without even checking to discover and know the truth, they spread those things and slander others and feel good or experience pleasure in doing it.

Also, if one has anger in heart, he will get angry at even small things. He will feel good only after he pours out anger. If he tries to hold back the rising anger, it is painful for him, so he cannot help but pour out anger.

In order to cast off these lusts of flesh, we have to pray. We can surely cast them off if we receive the fullness of the Spirit through fervent prayers. On the contrary, if we stop praying or lose the fullness of the Spirit, we give a chance to Satan to agitate the lust of flesh. As a result, we may commit sins in action.

1 Peter 5:8 says, *"Be of sober spirit, be on the alert. Your adversary, the devil, prowls around like a roaring lion, seeking someone to devour."* Through prayer, we always have to be awake to receive the fullness of the Holy Spirit. Through fervent prayers we can become poor in spirit by casting off the lust of the flesh, which is sinful nature.

Cast off the Lust of the Eyes

The lust of the eyes is the sinful nature that is agitated when we see or hear something. It moves us to desire and follow after what was seen or heard. When we see something, if we accept it along with feelings, when we see a similar thing later, it will stimulate similar feelings. Even without seeing, just by hearing something similar, a similar kind of feeling will arise, causing the lust of the eyes.

If we do not cut off but accept this lust of the eyes continually, it agitates the lust of the flesh. And again that finally is likely to lead to committing sins in action. David, who is a man after God's heart, also committed a sin due to the lust of the eyes.

One day, after David became the king and the nation came to have some stability, David was on the roof and by chance saw Bathsheba, Uriah's wife, bathing. He was tempted and took her and slept with her.

At that time, her husband was in the battlefield, fighting for the country. Later, David came to know that Bathsheba was pregnant. In order to conceal his wrongdoing, he called Uriah from the battlefield and urged him to sleep at home.

But in consideration of his fellow soldiers who were still fighting, he just slept at the door of the king's house. When things didn't turn out as he wanted, David sent Uriah to the frontlines of the battle for him to be killed.

David thought he loved God more than anybody else. Nevertheless, as the lust of the eyes came into him, he did the evil of sleeping with another man's wife. Furthermore, to conceal it, he committed the greater evil of murder.

Later, as retribution, he went through a great trial. The son born by Bathsheba died, and he had to escape from the rebellion of his son, Absalom. He even had to hear curses from a lowly person.

Through this, David was able to realize the form of evil in his heart and repented before God completely. Finally, he became a king who was greatly used by God.

These days, some young people enjoy adult materials in movies or on the Internet. But they should not take it lightly. This kind of the lust of the eyes is like igniting a fuse of the lust of the flesh.

Let us compare it with warfare. Suppose the lust of the flesh is represented by soldiers who are fighting within a walled city. Then the lust of the eyes is like reinforcements or military supplies to these soldiers inside the city wall. If they have constant supply, they will have greater strength to fight. If the lust of the flesh is reinforced we cannot win against it.

Therefore, since it is possible by our own will to cut off the lust of the eyes, we should not see, hear, or think anything that is not truth. Moreover, when we see, hear, and think only the truth and have only good feelings, we can cut off the lust of the eyes completely.

Cast off the Pride of this Life

The pride of this life is the nature that boasts of oneself. It is indulging in the physical pleasures of the world in order to satisfy the lust of the flesh and the lust of the eyes and to flaunt accomplishments before others. If we have this kind of nature, we will boast of wealth, honor, knowledge, talents, appearance and so on to reveal ourselves and get the attention of others.

James 4:16 says, *"But as it is, you boast in your arrogance; all such boasting is evil."* Boasting is of no benefit to us. Therefore, as said in 1 Corinthians 1:31, *"Let him who boasts, boast in the Lord,"* we have to boast only in the Lord to give God glory.

Boasting in the Lord is to boast of God answering us, giving us blessings and grace, and of the kingdom of heaven. It is to give glory to God and to plant faith and hope in the hearers so that they can long for spiritual things.

But some people say they are boasting in the Lord, but in a way they want to be lifted up through it. In this case, it cannot change others. Therefore, we should look back on ourselves in everything so that the pride of this life will not come upon us (Romans 15:2).

Become a Child Spiritually

There was a little child in a small town in the United States. Because the classroom of his Sunday school was very small, he began to pray to God to give them a bigger classroom. Even after several days, there was no answer, and then he began to write letters to God everyday.

However, even before he turned ten he died. As his mother was taking care of his belongings, she found the thick bundle of letters that he had written to God. She showed it to the pastor, and he was deeply touched. He talked about it in his sermon.

This news spread to many places, and offerings started to come from here and there and soon it was more than enough to build a new church. Later, an elementary school and high school were established in his name, and after that even a college. It was the result of the innocent faith of a young child who believed that God is the one who will give what we ask.

In Matthew chapter 18, the disciples asked Jesus who the greatest in the heavenly kingdom is. Jesus answered, *"Truly I say to you, unless you are converted and become like children, you will not enter the kingdom of heaven"* (v. 3). Before God, regardless of age, we all have to have the heart of children.

Children are innocent and pure, so they accept anything as they are taught. Likewise, only when we believe and obey the word of God as we hear and learn it can we enter into the heavenly kingdom.

For example, God's word says 'Pray continually,' and we should pray continually without giving an excuse. God tells us to rejoice always, and so, we always try to rejoice without thinking, 'How can I rejoice having these many sorrowful things in my life?' God tells us not to hate, and we try to love even our enemies without giving any excuses.

Likewise, if we have heart of children, we will quickly repent of what we have done wrong and try to live by the word of God.

But if a person is stained by the world and loses his innocence, he will be numb even when he commits sins. He will judge and condemn others, spread other people's faults and shortcomings, tell small and big lies, but will not even realize that he is doing evil things.

He will look down on others, try to be served, and if anything is not beneficial for him, he will just forget the grace that he received once. But he will not even have a guilty conscience. Because he has greater desire to seek his own, he will act in such a way to get it.

But in the truth, if we become a spiritual child, we will react sensitively about good and evil. If we see something good, we will be touched easily and shed tears, and we will hate and loathe what is evil.

Even if the people in the world say it is not evil, if God says it is evil, we will hate it from our heart and try not to commit any sin.

Also, a child is not arrogant, so he does not insist on his opinions. He just accepts what people teach him. Likewise, a spiritual child does not insist on his arrogance or try to be lifted up. Scribes and Pharisees at the time of Jesus judged and condemned others saying they knew the truth, but a spiritual child will not do such a thing. He will only act humbly and gently like our Lord.

So, a spiritual child does not insist that he is right when he listens to the word of God. Even though there is something that is not in agreement with his knowledge or something that he does not understand, he will not judge or misunderstand, but just believe and obey first. When he hears about the works of God, he will not show any pride or arrogance but long to experience the same kinds of works himself, too.

If we become spiritual children, we will believe and obey the word of God as it is. If we find any sin at all according to the word, we will try to change ourselves.

But in some cases, they lead a Christian life for a long time, and they just store the word of God as knowledge, and their heart becomes that of an adult. When they first received God's grace, they repented and fasted to cast off their sins that they found out, but later, they become numb.

When they listen to the word, they think, "I know this." Or, they obey just the things that are beneficial for them or the things that they can agree with. They judge and condemn others with the word they know.

Therefore, to become poor in spirit, we always have to find the evil in us through the word, cast it off through fervent prayer, and become spiritual children. Only then will we be able to enjoy all the blessings that God has prepared for us.

Blessing to Possess the Eternal Kingdom of Heaven

Then, specifically, what kinds of blessings those who are poor in spirit will receive? Matthew 5:3 says, *"Blessed are the poor in spirit, for theirs is the kingdom of heaven,"* and as said, they will receive true and eternal blessing, namely the kingdom of heaven.

The heavenly kingdom is where the children of God will dwell. It is a spiritual place that cannot be compared with this world. Just as parents wait for their baby to be born and prepare all things such as toys and a baby carriage, God is preparing the kingdom of heaven for those who are poor in spirit, open their heart, and accept the gospel to become His children.

As Jesus said, *"In My Father's house are many dwelling places"* (John 14:2), there are many dwelling places in the heavenly kingdom. According to how much we love God and live by His word to keep our faith, the dwelling places in heaven will be different.

If one is poor in spirit, but just remains at the level of accepting Jesus Christ and receiving salvation, he will go into Paradise to live there forever. But as one goes on in his life in Christ and changes himself by the word of God, then the First, Second, and Third Kingdoms of Heaven will be given. Furthermore, he who has accomplished sanctification of heart and has been faithful in all God's house will receive the most beautiful dwelling place, New Jerusalem, to enjoy eternal blessings.

Please refer to books *Heaven I* and *Heaven II* about the dwelling places and happy life in the heavenly kingdom. Here, let me introduce to you just a little bit about the life of New Jerusalem.

In the City of New Jerusalem, where the light of God's glory is shining, the sound of praise of angels is faintly heard. A golden road runs between the buildings that are built with gold and precious stones that give out brilliant lights. Perfectly landscaped green fields, lawns, trees, and beautiful flowers are well-blended.

The river of water of life, which is clear as crystal, flows quietly. Fine golden sands lie on the riverbanks. On golden benches are placed baskets that contain fruits from the tree of life. In the far distance one can see the sea like glass. On the sea, there is a splendid cruise ship that is made with many kinds of jewels.

People who enter into this place are ministered to by numerous angels, and they enjoy the authority of a king. They can fly into the sky riding shining cloud-like-automobiles. They always see the Lord in close proximity and enjoy heavenly banquets with famous prophets.

Additionally, in New Jerusalem there are countless valuable and beautiful things that we cannot see on this earth. Every corner is scenery that enraptures the senses.

Therefore, we should not just remain at the level of barely receiving salvation, but have more of poor spirit and change ourselves completely with the word, so that we will enter into the City of New Jerusalem, the most beautiful dwelling place in heaven.

The Nearness of God is Our Blessing

When we become poor in spirit, we will not just meet God and receive salvation, but also we will receive the authority as the children of God and other blessings. Let me introduce to you the testimony of an elder in the church. He had suffered from 'pollution disease' or otherwise called 'public hazard disease,' but received the blessings of being poor in spirit.

About ten years ago, he had to take a temporary rest from his job due to the disease. Many times he had the urge to end his life due to the serious feeling of helplessness. Since he couldn't see any light of hope and knowing that he couldn't do anything by himself, he had poor spirit.

In the meantime, he went to a bookstore, and by chance, one book came into his sight. It was the *Tasting Eternal Life before Death*. It is the book about my testimony and memoirs. I had been an atheist, and I was wandering around the threshold of death due to the seven-year long period of diseases that couldn't be cured by any human method. But God came to me and met me.

The man felt my life was very similar to his, and he bought the book feeling that he was being drawn by some kind of force. He read it overnight and shed so many tears. He was assured that he could also be healed and registered in our church.

Since then, he got healed of his peculiar disease by the

power of God, and he was able to return to work. He has been commended by both many of his colleagues and his superiors. He has received blessings of being promoted. Furthermore, he evangelized more than seventy people among his relatives. How great his heavenly reward will be!

Psalm 73:28 says, *"But as for me, the nearness of God is my good; I have made the LORD God my refuge, that I may tell of all Your works."*

If we have taken the first blessing among the Beatitudes by being near God, we should become more spiritual children, love God more passionately, and preach the gospel to those who are poor in spirit. I hope you will completely possess the Beatitudes that the God of love and blessings has prepared for you.

Chapter 2
The Second Blessing

Blessed Are Those Who Mourn, for They Shall Be Comforted

Matthew 5:4

*"Blessed are those who mourn,
for they shall be comforted."*

There were two friends who loved each other very much. They cared for and loved each other so much that they could even sacrifice their lives to save the other. But one day, one of them died in a battle. The one who was left mourned until evening, missing the friend who was gone.

"I am distressed for you, my brother Jonathan; you have been very pleasant to me. Your love to me was more wonderful than the love of women."

This man took the son of his friend and cared for him like his own son. It is the story of David and Jonathan, explained in 2 Samuel chapter 1.

While we are living in this world, we face many sad things like death of loved ones, pains of diseases, troubles in lives, financial problems, and so on. It is not an exaggeration to say that life is a continuation of sorrow.

Fleshly Mourning, Not the Will of God

In human history, we find wars, terrorism, famine, and other disasters which take place at national levels. Also, there are many sorrowful things and problems taking place at the individual level.

Some are in sorrow because of financial difficulties, and some others suffer from the pains of sicknesses. Some have broken hearts because their plans are not fulfilled and others shed bitter tears having been betrayed by their loved ones.

This kind of mourning caused by sorrowful occurrences is fleshly mourning. It comes from one's evil emotions. It is never the will of God. This kind of fleshly mourning cannot be comforted by God.

But rather, the Bible tells us that it is the will of God for us to rejoice always (1 Thessalonians 5:16). Also, God tells us in Philippians 4:4, *"Rejoice in the Lord always; again I will say, rejoice!"* Many Bible verses tell us to rejoice.

Some may wonder thinking, "I can rejoice when I have something to rejoice, but while I am suffering from so many troubles, pains, and hardships, how can I rejoice?"

But we can rejoice and give thanks because we have already become God's children who are saved and received the promise of the heavenly kingdom. Also, as God's children, when we ask, He will hear and solve our problems. Because we believe this fact, we can surely rejoice and give thanks.

It is the story of Rev. Dr. Myong-ho Cheong, who is a missionary to Africa from our church, preaching the gospel in so many meetings in fifty-four African countries. About ten years ago, he quit his job as a college professor and went to Africa for missionary works. Soon, his only son died.

Many church members comforted him, but he only gave thanks to God and rather comforted the church members. He was thankful because God had taken his son to the heavenly kingdom where there is no tear, sorrow, pain, or disease, and because he had the hope to see his son again in heaven, he could rejoice.

Likewise, if we have faith, we will not have fleshly mourning being unable to overcome our sad emotions because of some sorrowful things. We will be able to rejoice in any situation.

Even if we encounter a certain problem, if we give thanks and pray with faith, God works seeing our faith. He will work for the good of everything, and thus, to true children of God, physically sorrowful situations will not matter.

God Wants Spiritual Mourning

What God wants is not fleshly mourning but spiritual mourning. Matthew 5:4 says, *"Blessed are those who mourn,"* and here 'mourning' means spiritual mourning for the kingdom and righteousness of God. Then, what kinds of spiritual mourning are there?

First there is the mourning of repentance.

When we believe in Jesus Christ and accept Him as our Savior, we realize from heart, by the help of the Holy Spirit, that He died on the cross for our sins. When we feel this love of Jesus, we will have the mourning of repentance, repenting of our sins with tears and runny nose.

Repentance is to turn back from living in sins and to live by the word of God. When we have the mourning of repentance, the burden of our sins will be taken away, and we can experience that joy overflows from our heart.

It's already more than thirty years ago, but I still clearly remember the first revival meeting I attended after meeting God. There, I had so much mourning of repentance with tears and runny nose, hearing the word of God.

Even before I met God, I took pride in myself that I lived a righteous and good life. But listening to the word of God, looking back on my past life, I found there were so many untruthful things. When I tore my heart in repentance, my body felt so light and refreshed like it was flying. I also gained confidence that I could live by the word of God. From that time on I quit smoking and drinking and began to read the Bible and attend dawn prayer meetings.

Even after receiving this grace of having mourning of repentance, we may have other things to mourn for in our Christian lives. Once we have become God's children, we have to cast off sins and live a holy life according to the word of God. But until we reach a grown up measure of faith, we are not yet perfect and we sometimes commit sins.

In this situation, if we love God, we will feel so sorry before

God and repent thoroughly praying, "God, help me so that this kind of thing will never happen again. Give me the strength to practice Your word." When we have this kind of mourning, the strength to cast off sins will come from above. Thus, how great a blessing it is to mourn!

Some believers repeatedly commit the same sins and repent again and again. It is a case where change is very slow or where there is no change. It's because they do not really repent from the bottom of their heart, although they may say they have mourning of repentance.

Suppose a young person is hanging out with bad friends and does a lot of bad things. He asks for forgiveness from his parents, but keeps on doing the same things. Then, it is not true repentance. He has to turn away, stop hanging out with bad friends and study hard. Only then can it be considered true repentance.

Likewise, we should not keep on committing the same sins, just repenting with words, but bear the fruit of repentance by showing the right deeds (Luke 3:8).

Furthermore, as our faith grows up and we become leaders in the church, we should not have any mourning of repentance any longer. This does not mean we should not mourn even after committing sins. It means we have to cast off sins so that there won't be anything to mourn about.

When we do not fulfill our duties, we also mourn in

repentance. 1 Corinthians 4:2 says, *"In this case, moreover, it is required of stewards that one be found trustworthy."* So, we have to be faithful and bear good fruits in our duties. If we don't, we have to have the mourning of repentance.

One important thing here is that if we do not repent and turn back when we don't fulfill our duties, it can become a wall of sin against God, and consequently we will not be protected by God. It is something like an older child who is still acting like a baby, and he has to be scolded all the time.

But if we repent and mourn from the bottom of our heart, God-given joy and peace will come on us. God will also give us the confidence that we can do it. He gives us the strength to fulfill our duties. This is the comfort that God is giving to those who mourn.

Next, there is the mourning for brothers in faith.

Sometimes, brothers in faith commit sins and go the way of death. In this case, if we have mercy, we will have anxiety and concern for those brothers. So, we will mourn as if it were our own matters. We will even repent on behalf of them and pray with love so that they can act by the truth.

We can have this kind of mourning and tearful prayers of repenting on behalf of them, only when we have true love for those souls. God delights with this kind of prayer with mourning and gives us His comfort.

On the contrary, there are people who judge and condemn others, and give hard times to others rather than mourning and praying for them. Also, some people spread iniquities of other people, and this is not right in the sight of God. We have to cover the faults of others with love, and pray for them not to commit sin.

The martyrdom of Stephen is recorded in Acts chapter 7. The Jews were offended by the message that Stephen preached. When he said that his spiritual eyes were opened and he saw the Lord Jesus standing on the right hand of God, they stoned him to death.

Even while he was being stoned, Stephen prayed with love for those evil people who were stoning him.

> *They went on stoning Stephen as he called on the Lord and said, 'Lord Jesus, receive my spirit!' Then falling on his knees, he cried out with a loud voice, 'Lord, do not hold this sin against them!' Having said this, he fell asleep (Acts 7:59-60).*

What were the actions of Jesus like? He received all the mockery and persecutions when He was crucified, yet He prayed for those who were crucifying Him, saying, *"Father, forgive them; for they do not know what they are doing"* (Luke 23:34).

While taking the pains of the cross and though He was

totally innocent, He still prayed for the forgiveness of sins of those who were crucifying Him. Through this, we can understand how deep, wide and great the love of Jesus is for the souls. This is the proper kind of heart in the sight of God. It is the heart with which we can receive blessings.

There is also mourning to save more souls.

When God's children see those who are being stained by the sin of this world and going on the path of destruction, they must have loving compassion desiring mercy for them. Today, sin and evil prevail just like in the time of Noah. That generation was punished by flood. Sodom and Gomorrah were punished by fire.

Therefore, we should have the mourning for our parents, brothers and sisters, relatives, and neighbors who are not yet saved. Also, we should mourn for our nation and people, the churches, and about things that disturb the kingdom of God. This means we should have the mourning for saving souls.

The apostle Paul always worried and mourned for the kingdom and righteousness of God and the souls. He was persecuted and went through so many hardships preaching the gospel. He was even jailed. But he did not mourn for his personal suffering, but only praised and prayed to God (Acts 16:25). But for the kingdom of God and the souls, he mourned ever so greatly.

Apart from such external things, there is the daily

pressure on me of concern for all the churches. Who is weak without my being weak? Who is led into sin without my intense concern? (2 Corinthians 11:28-29)

Therefore be on the alert, remembering that night and day for a period of three years I did not cease to admonish each one with tears (Acts 20:31).

When the believers do not stand firmly on the word of God or when the church does not reveal the glory of God, people like Paul will mourn and have worried concerns for it.

Also, when they are persecuted for the name of the Lord, they do not mourn because it is hard for them. They rather mourn for the souls of the other people. Furthermore, when they see the world is becoming more and more darkened, they mourn and pray that the glory of God will be revealed more greatly and more souls will be saved.

The Need for Spiritual Love to Spiritually Mourn

Now, what should we do to mourn spiritually, which is what God wants? To have spiritual mourning, above all, we have to have spiritual love in us.

As said in John 6:63, *"It is the Spirit who gives life; the flesh profits nothing,"* only the kind of love that God recognizes gives life and is able to lead people in the way of salvation. Even if one seems to have a lot of love, if his love is far removed from the truth, it is only fleshly love.

Love can be categorized into fleshly love and spiritual love. Fleshly love is the love that seeks one's own. It is meaningless love that finally changes and perishes. On the other hand, spiritual love never changes. This is love within the word of God that is the truth. It is true love that seeks the benefit of the other while sacrificing oneself.

Spiritual love cannot be possessed by men's strength. Only when we realize the love of God and dwell in the truth can we give such love. If we have spiritual love that is the love that can love even our enemies and give up our lives for others, then God will give us abundant blessings. With this love, we can give life wherever we go, and many people will return to the Lord.

Therefore, when we have spiritual love in our heart, we can mourn for dying souls and pray for them. With this love, even people with hardened hearts will be changed, and it can give life and faith.

The patriarchs of faith who were loved by God had this kind of spiritual love, and they prayed for the souls who were going the way of destruction. They prayed with tears and mourning for the kingdom and righteousness of God. They did not just shed tears, but they took care of other souls day and night, being faithful to the duties given to them.

It is truly spiritual mourning only when it is followed by deeds of preaching the word, praying, and taking care of the souls with love for them. If we have spiritual love, we will also have spiritual mourning for God's kingdom and His righteousness.

Then, as said in Matthew 6:33, *"But seek first His kingdom and His righteousness, and all these things will be added to you,"* the spirit and soul will change, the kingdom of God will be accomplished, and other necessary things will be abundantly supplied by God.

The Blessings Given to Those Who Mourn

As said in Matthew 5:4, *"Blessed are those who mourn, for they shall be comforted,"* if we mourn spiritually, we will be comforted by God.

The comfort that God gives us is different from the comfort that people can give. 1 John 3:18 says, *"Little children, let us not love with word or with tongue, but in deed and truth."* As God has spoken, He does not comfort us with just words alone but with material things as well.

To those who are poor, God gives them financial blessings. To those who suffer from illnesses, God gives them health. To those who pray for heart's desires, God gives the answer.

Also, to those who are mourning because they don't have enough strength to fulfill their duties, God gives the strength. To those who mourn for the souls, God gives them the fruit of evangelism and revival. Furthermore, to those who tear their heart and mourn to cast off sins, God gives them the grace of the forgiveness of sins. Also, to the extent that they cast off sins and become sanctified, God blesses them to manifest great and powerful works of God as done in the case of the apostle Paul.

Several years ago, I went through great difficulties in which the existence of this church was threatened. I had to mourn so much because of the people who brought trials to the church, and for those members who were innocent and still being persecuted. Because of the members who had weak faith and left church, I couldn't even eat or sleep.

Because I knew what a great sin it was to disturb the church of God, I shed so many tears thinking of the souls that brought troubles to the church. Especially, when I saw the souls who just heard false rumors, left church and stood against God, I had to mourn so much feeling the responsibility of not having taken care of them properly.

I lost so much weight, and it was difficult for me to even walk. I still had to preach three times a week. Sometimes my body was shaking, but because of my concern for the church members, I had to stay in my place. God saw this heart of mine and whenever I prayed, He comforted me saying, "I love you. This is rather a blessing."

The Blessing to Receive God's Comfort

When the time came, God solved each of the misunderstandings one by one, and it was the chance for our church members to grow up in faith. God began to show such amazing works of His power that could not compare with anything previously. He showed us numerous signs and wonders and extraordinary things.

He saved the church from collapse and He gave us blessings of church revival instead. He also widely opened the way of the world mission. In overseas crusades, He sent hundreds, then thousands and millions of people to gather and hear the gospel and receive salvation. What kind of reward and joy it was!

The '2002 India Miracle Healing Prayer Festival' was held on the second longest beach in the world, Marina Beach, India. It was attended by an estimated total number of more than 3 million people. Many of them were healed and numerous Hindus converted.

God's comfort comes in blessings that we cannot imagine. He gives us what we need the most, and more than enough. He also gives us rewards in the heavenly kingdom, and therefore it is the true blessing.

Revelation 21:4 says, *"He will wipe away every tear from their eyes; and there will no longer be any death; there will no longer be any mourning, or crying, or pain; the first things have passed away."* As spoken, God pays back to us with glory and rewards in heaven where there is no tear, no sorrow, and no pain.

The heavenly houses of those who always mourn and pray for the kingdom of God and His church will have possessions of gold, many precious stones and other rewards. And especially, it will be decorated with big and shining pearls. Until each pearl is made, the oyster has to endure pain and agitation for a long time and secrete a crystalline substance, giving up of itself to form the pearl.

In the same way, while we are being cultivated on this earth, if we shed tears to change, and pray with mourning for the kingdom of God and other souls, God will comfort us with the pearl symbolizing all these things.

Therefore, let us not mourn in a fleshly way, but spiritually and only for the kingdom of God and for other souls. In doing so we will be comforted by God and receive valuable rewards in the heavenly kingdom as well.

Chapter 3
The Third Blessing

Blessed Are the Gentle, for They Shall Inherit the Earth

Matthew 5:5

Blessed are the gentle,
for they shall inherit the earth.

When Lincoln was an unknown lawyer in his younger years, there was a lawyer by the name of Edwin M. Stanton who disliked Lincoln very much. Once, Stanton was told that he had to take a case with Lincoln, and he slammed the door and left.

"How am I supposed to work with this countryside lawyer?"

After time passed, when the president-elect Lincoln was forming his cabinet, he appointed Stanton as the twenty-seventh United States Secretary of War. Lincoln's advisers were surprised and asked him to reconsider his appointment. It was because Stanton had once publically criticized Lincoln saying that it was a "national disaster" that Lincoln had been elected as the president.

"What's the matter even if he looks down on me? He has a great sense of duty and he has the ability to overcome difficult situations. He is more than qualified to be the Secretary of War."

Lincoln had a heart that was both broad and meek. He was able to understand and embrace even a person who was criticizing him. Finally, even Stanton came to respect him and when he died, he remarked of Lincoln, saying, "Lincoln was the most perfect ruler of men the world has ever seen."

Likewise, rather than disliking and avoiding a person who does not like us, to change him and to bring out his good points is demonstrating a good and gentle heart.

Spiritual Gentleness Acknowledged by God

Generally, people say that being introversive, timid, meek and having a mild and soft temperament is to be gentle. But God says those who are gentle with virtue are really gentle.

Here 'virtue' means 'things that are right, proper and of an upright heart.' Having virtue in God is to act uprightly in exercising control with other people, to have dignity, and being equipped in all aspects.

Gentleness and virtue seem to be similar, but there is a clear difference. The gentleness is more inward while the virtue is like the clothing on the outside. Even if one is a great person, if he does not wear proper clothes, it will bring down his projection of elegance and dignity. Similarly, if we do not have virtue along with gentleness, it cannot be perfection. Also, even if we seem to have virtue, if we do not have the gentleness inside, it is valueless. It is like a nutshell without anything inside.

The spiritual gentleness that can be acknowledged by God is not just having mild character; it is to also have virtue. Then, we will be able to have broad heart to embrace many people like a big tree gives a big shadow for the people to rest.

Because Jesus was gentle, He did not quarrel or cry out, and His sound was not heard on the street. He treated good men and evil men with the same heart, and so, many people followed Him.

Virtue to Embrace Many People

In Korea's history, there was a king who had gentle character. It was Sejong the Great. He not only had a gentle character but he also possessed virtue. He was loved by his ministers and the people. In his time, there were great scholars like Hwang Hee and Maeng Sa Sung. Most importantly, he had the achievement of creating 'Han-gul,' the Korean alphabet.

He reformed the medical system and also metal type set. He appointed many kinds of people in various areas including music and science, and accomplished splendid cultural achievements. So you see that if one possesses gentleness with virtue, many people can rest in him, and the fruit is also beautiful.

Those who are gentle can embrace even others who have different ideas and educations. They don't judge or condemn with evil in any matter. They understand from the other's point of view in any situation. Their hearts can be described as soft and comfortable enough to serve others in humbleness.

If we throw a stone onto a piece of hard metal, it will create a loud noise. If we throw a stone at glass, it will shatter. But if we throw a stone into a bundle of cotton, it won't make noise or break, because the cotton will embrace the stone.

Likewise, he who is gentle will not forsake even those who have weak faith and are acting in evil. He will wait until the end for them to change and guide them to do better. His words will not be loud or shattering, but soft and gentle. He will not speak meaningless things but only words of truth that are necessary.

Also, even if some others hate him, he will not be offended or have ill-feelings against them. When he receives advice or reprimand, he will accept it joyfully to improve himself. This kind of person will not have any trouble with any other person. He will understand the shortcomings of others and embrace them, so that he will gain the hearts of the many.

Cultivate the Heart and Make it Good Soil

In order for us to have spiritual gentleness, we have to try to diligently cultivate the field of our heart. In Matthew chapter 13, Jesus gave us the parable of four different kinds of soil, likening them to our heart.

In the soil along the hardened pathway, any seed that has fallen on it will not be able to sprout and take root. A heart like this will not have faith even after listening to the word of God. One who has this kind of heart is stubborn; he does not open his heart even after hearing the truth, so he cannot meet God. Even if he may be attending church, he is just a churchgoer. The word is not planted in him, so his faith cannot sprout, take root and grow.

The rocky field may sprout the seed fallen on it, but a crop from the seed cannot grow because of the rocks. One who has this heart does not have assurance of faith even after listening to the word. When tested, he fails and falls. He knows God and also receives the fullness of the Spirit, so he is better than the soil 'along the path.' But, because his heart is not cultivated in the truth, it withers and dies and there are no deeds that follow cultivation.

In the thorny field, the seed can sprout and grow up, but because of the thorns, it cannot bear fruit. One who has this heart has his desires, temptations for money, worries of this world and his own plans and thoughts, so he cannot experience the power of God in every matter.

In the good soil, the seed can grow up and bear fruit that is thirty, sixty, or one-hundred times more than the original seed. One who has this heart will obey only with 'Yes' and 'Amen' to the word of God he hears, so he can bear abundant fruit in each and every matter. This is the kind of heart of goodness that God desires.

Let us check what kind of heart we have. Of course, it is difficult to make exact distinction among different hearts, whether along the path, in rocky soil, in the thorny field, or in good soil as if we were measuring it with a scale. The 'along the path' can also have some rocky soil, and even if we have some good soil, untruths that are like rocks can be put in our heart as we grow.

But regardless of the kind of heart soil we have, if we diligently cultivate it, we can make it good soil. Similarly, rather than what kind of heart we have, the more important thing is how diligently we try to cultivate our heart.

Just as a farmer takes out the rocks, pulls out the weeds, and fertilizes the soil to make it good soil while hoping for an abundant harvest, if we remove the forms of evil like hatred, envy, jealousy, quarrels, judging, and condemning from our heart, we can have good heart-soil that is rich in goodness and gentle in character.

Pray with Faith until the End and Cast off Evil

In order for us to cultivate our heart, first of all, we first have to worship in spirit and in truth to listen to the word and understand it. Also, even in difficulties, we have to rejoice always, pray continually, and give thanks in all circumstances along with the effort to cast off the evils in our heart.

If we ask for the strength of God through fervent prayer and try to live by the word, then, we can receive the grace and strength of God and the help of the Holy Spirit, so that we can quickly cast off evil.

Even if the soil is very good, if we do not sow the seeds and do not take care of the crop, then, we won't have any harvest. Likewise, the important thing is that we should not try once or twice and then stop, but pray with faith until the end. Because faith is the substance of things hoped for (Hebrews 11:1), we have to diligently try and pray with faith. Only then will we be able to reap abundantly.

Also, in the process of casting off the forms of evil from our hearts, we may think we have cast off evil to some extent, but then it may seem that the evil just keeps surfacing. It's just like when we peel the skin off onions. Even after peeling off the layers a couple of times, it still has the same kind of skin. But if we do not give up but keep on casting off evil to the end, we will finally have gentle heart that has no evil in it.

Gentleness of Moses

While Moses was leading the Israelites to the land of Canaan during the forty years of the Exodus, he encountered so many difficult situations.

Only adult men were 600,000. Including women and children, the number must have exceeded two million people. He had to guide so many people for forty years in the wilderness where there was no food or water. We can imagine how many difficult obstacles he must have had to overcome!

There was the army of Egypt following them behind (Exodus 14:9), and in their front was the Red Sea. But God opened the Red Sea for them so that they could cross it like dry land (Exodus 14:21-22).

When there was no drinking water, God caused water to flow out from rock (Exodus 17:6). God also changed bitter water into sweet water (Exodus 15:23-25). When there was no food, God sent manna and quail to feed them (Exodus chapter 14-17).

Even when they were witnessing the power of the living God, the Israelites complained against Moses each time they had a difficulty.

> *The sons of Israel said to them, "Would that we had died by the LORD's hand in the land of Egypt, when we sat by the pots of meat, when we ate bread to the full; for you have brought us out into this wilderness to kill this whole assembly with hunger" (Exodus 16:3).*

> *But the people thirsted there for water; and they grumbled against Moses and said, "Why, now, have you brought us up from Egypt, to kill us and our children and our livestock with thirst?" (Exodus 17:3)*

> *You grumbled in your tents and said, "Because the LORD hates us, He has brought us out of the land of Egypt to deliver us into the hand of the Amorites to destroy us" (Deuteronomy 1:27).*

Some of them even tried to stone Moses. Moses had to stay with this kind of people for forty years, teaching them with the truth and leading them to the land of Canaan. Just with this fact alone, we can imagine the level of his gentleness.

That is why God praised him in Numbers 12:3 KJV, saying, *"Now the man Moses was very meek, above all the men which were upon the face of the earth."*

But it's not that Moses had such gentleness from the beginning. He had the temper to kill an Egyptian who was abusing a Hebrew man. He also had great confidence in having been a prince of Egypt. But he humbled himself and lowered himself completely while he was tending the flocks in the desert of Midian for forty years.

Because of his killing of an Egyptian, he had to leave the palace of the Pharaoh and became a fugitive. He finally came to realize that he couldn't do anything with his own power while he was living in the wilderness. But, after spending this time in refinement, he became such a gentle person that he was capable of embracing anybody.

Difference between Fleshly and Spiritual Gentleness

Usually, those who are gentle in a fleshly sense are quiet and timid in character. They don't want any kind of loud noises or crashing sounds.

So, we may see that they are somewhat indecisive even with

untruths. When they have some uncomfortable situations, they may suppress it inside, but they suffer in heart. When a situation exceeds the limit of what they can tolerate, they may explode to surprise many people. Also, in their duties, they don't have the passion to be faithful so in the end they do not bear fruit.

In this way being timid and introversive in character is not the kind of gentleness with which God delights. Men may think this is gentleness, but in the sight of God, who searches the heart, this character cannot be recognized as gentleness.

But those who accomplish spiritual gentleness of the heart by casting off untruths from the heart will bear abundant fruits in different aspects of evangelism and revival, just as good soil can produce an abundant harvest.

Also, spiritually, they will bear the fruit of the Light (Ephesians 5:9), fruits of spiritual love (1 Corinthians chapter 13:4-7), and the fruit of the Holy Spirit (Galatians 5:22-23). This way, they become a man of spirit, so they quickly receive answers to their prayers.

Above all, those who are spiritually gentle are strong and brave in the truth. When they have to teach with the truth, they can be stern in teaching. When they see those souls who commit sins before God, they can also have the strength and boldness to rebuke and correct with love whoever it might be.

For example, Jesus is the most gentle of all, but about the things that were not right according to the truth, He rebuked the people harshly. That is, He did not tolerate defiling the Temple of God.

> And He found in the temple those who were selling oxen and sheep and doves, and the money changers seated at their tables. And He made a scourge of cords, and drove them all out of the temple, with the sheep and the oxen; and He poured out the coins of the money changers and overturned their tables; and to those who were selling the doves He said, "Take these things away; stop making My Father's house a place of business" (John 2:14-16).

He also sternly rebuked the Pharisees and scribes who were teaching in untruth, going against the word of God (Matthew 12:34; 23:13-35; Luke 11:42-44).

Level of Spiritual Gentleness

One thing we should know is that there is gentleness in spiritual love of 1 Corinthians chapter 13, and also spiritual gentleness that is among the nine fruits of the Holy Spirit in Galatians chapter 5.
Then, how are they different from the gentleness in the Beatitudes? Of course, the three things are not completely different. The basic meaning is to be soft and mild while

having love and virtue. But the depth and width of each one is different.

First, the gentleness in spiritual love is the most basic level of gentleness to accomplish love. The gentleness in the nine fruits of the Holy Spirit has a broader meaning; it is the gentleness in every matter.

The gentleness in the fruits of the Spirit is what is born as fruit in the heart, and when this fruit is put in effect and brings down blessings, then this is the gentleness in the Beatitudes.

For example, we can say that when we have good fruits abundantly on a beautiful tree, we call it the "fruit of the Holy Spirit," but when we take the fruit to benefit our body, it is the fruit in the Beatitudes. Therefore, we can say that the gentleness in the Beatitudes is of the higher level.

Blessings Given to the Spiritually Gentle

As said in Matthew 5:5, *"Blessed are the gentle, for they shall inherit the earth,"* if we have spiritual gentleness, we will inherit the earth.

Here, 'inheriting the earth' does not mean we will receive the land on this earth, but we will possess the land in the eternal kingdom of heaven (Psalm 37:29).

An inheritance is the acquisition of a possession, condition, or trait from past generations. The ownership of an inheritance is usually more recognized by others than that of other properties that are bought with money.

For example, if a person has a piece of land that has been passed down in the family for many generations, it is already known to all the neighbors. The family will keep it as something precious and pass it down to their children. Therefore, to inherit the earth means we will receive it as our land for sure.

Then, what is the reason that God gives the land in the heavenly kingdom to those who have spiritual gentleness? Psalm 37:11 NKJV says, *"But the meek shall inherit the earth, and shall delight themselves in the abundance of peace."* As said, it's because those who are gentle have virtue and embrace many people.

He who has gentleness can forgive the faults of others, understand them and embrace them, so that many people can find rest in him and enjoy peace in him.

When a person gains the heart of the many, it becomes the spiritual authority for him, and even in the heavenly kingdom, he will receive great authority. Thus, he will naturally inherit great land.

Spiritual Authority to Inherit the Land in the Heavenly Kingdom

In this world, one can gain authority only when he has wealth and fame, but in the heavenly kingdom, spiritual authority is given to those who humble themselves and serve others.

Matthew 20:26-28 says, *"It is not this way among you, but whoever wishes to become great among you shall be your servant, and whoever wishes to be first among you shall be your slave; just as the Son of Man did not come to be served, but to serve, and to give His life a ransom for many."*

Matthew 18:3-4 says, *"Truly I say to you, unless you are converted and become like children, you will not enter the kingdom of heaven. Whoever then humbles himself as this child, he is the greatest in the kingdom of heaven."*

If we become like children, our hearts will be humbled to the lowest possible. So that we will gain the heart of many people on this earth, and we will become those who are the great in heaven.

Likewise, since one embraces the heart of many people with spiritual gentleness, God gives vast areas of land accordingly to let him enjoy his authority forever. If we do not gain vast lands in heaven, how can great and excellent homes be built?

Suppose we have done many works for God and received many materials to build our house in heaven, but if we have only a small portion of land, we cannot build such a big house.

Therefore, those who go into New Jerusalem will be given big parcels of land because they will have accomplished spiritual gentleness completely. Since their portion of land is big, their houses will also be big and beautiful.

Also, for each home, in the most suitable way, there will be natural facilities like beautifully maintained gardens, lakes, valleys, and hills. There will also be other facilities like swimming pools, playgrounds, ballrooms, etc. This is God's care for the house owner to invite those whom he has embraced and helped them grow in spirit and have banquets and share their love eternally.

Even today, God is diligently looking for those who are gentle. It is to give them duties to embrace so many souls and lead them to the truth, and to give them vast portions of the land as inheritances in the eternal kingdom of heaven. Therefore, let us diligently accomplish sanctification and gentleness of heart, so that we will be able to inherit vast the land in the kingdom of heaven.

Chapter 4
The Fourth Blessing

Blessed Are Those Who Hunger and Thirst for Righteousness, for They Shall Be Satisfied

Matthew 5:6

Blessed are those who hunger and thirst for righteousness, for they shall be satisfied.

A Korean saying goes, "One will become a thief if he goes without eating for three days." It tells us of the pain of being hungry. Even the strongest man cannot do anything if he is hunger-stricken.

It's not easy to skip just a couple of meals, and imagine what it would be like if you cannot eat for one, two, or three days.

First, you feel that you are hungry, but when more time passes, you get a stomachache, and you may also have cold sweats. You will start to ache all over your body and your body functions will deteriorate. Your desire for food will become extreme in this situation. If it continues, you may even lose your life.

Even today, there are people suffering from severe famine and in wars who even eat poisonous plants. There are many who continue to live from day to day by finding something to eat in garbage cans and in piles of trash.

But, what is more unbearable than hunger is thirst. It is commonly known that 70% of human body is water. If we lose just 2% of the liquid in the body, we will have serious thirst. If we lose 4%, the body will become weak, and we may even lose consciousness. If we lose 10%, we may die.

Water is an absolutely essential element for the human body. Because of extreme thirst, some people who travel across the desert under the scorching sun will follow a mirage thinking they see an oasis, and lose their lives.

This way, to have hunger and thirst is a genuinely painful thing, and it can even take our lives. Then, why does God say blessed are those who hunger and thirst for righteousness?

Those who Hunger and Thirst for Righteousness

Righteousness is the noun for being righteous, which *The Merriam-Webster's Online Dictionary* defines as 'acting in accord with divine or moral law: free from guilt or sin.' Around us, we may see some people who even sacrifice their lives to keep a wrong kind of righteousness between friends. They also protest against the social irregularities insisting their belief is the righteousness.

But God's righteousness is something different. It is to follow the will of God and to practice the word of God who is the goodness and truth itself. It refers to every step that we have to take until we completely recover the lost image of God, and become sanctified.

Those who hunger and thirst for righteousness will delight in the Law of the LORD God and meditate on it day and night as written in Psalm 1:1-2. It's because the word of God contains what the will of God is and what kinds of deeds are righteous deeds.

Also, just like the confession of the Psalmist, they will long for the word of God and take it day and night. It's not just to store it as knowledge but to apply it in their lives.

My eyes fail with longing for Your salvation and for Your righteous word (Psalm 119:123).

I rise before dawn and cry for help; I wait for Your words. My eyes anticipate the night watches, that I may meditate on Your word (Psalm 119:147-148).

If we truly know the love of God, we will earnestly long for His word, thus hungering and thirsting for righteousness. It's because, we understand that the one and only Son of God, Jesus, who was blameless and spotless, took the sufferings and shame of the cross for us. He took the shame and suffering of the cross to redeem us, who were all sinners, from our sins and give us eternal life.

If we believe this love of the cross, we cannot but live by the word of God. We will think, 'How can I pay back the love of the Lord and please God? How can I do what God wants?' Like a thirsty deer looks for stream of water, we will seek the kind of righteousness that God wants.

Thus, we will diligently obey as we hear the word, cast off sins, and practice the truth.

Deeds of Those who Hunger and Thirst for Righteousness

By the power of God, I was healed of so many diseases that

medicine could not cure. As I met God this way, I longed for the word of God who gave me a new life. To hear more and understand more, I attended every revival meeting and sought God to meet Him more closely.

> *I love those who love me; and those who diligently seek me will find me (Proverbs 8:17).*

As I realized the will of God through sermons about keeping the whole Sabbath, giving proper tithes, and that we should not come before God empty-handed (Exodus 23:15), I tried to practice the word diligently. With my thanks to God who healed me and saved me, I was thirsty to practice the word of God.

As the process to practice the righteousness of God began, I realized that I had hatred in my heart. Then I thought, "What am I that I have the capacity to hate somebody?"

I had hatred against those who hurt my feelings while I was on my sickbed for seven years, but as I realized the love of Jesus, who was crucified and shed His blood and water for me, I prayed hard to cast off hatred.

> *Call to Me and I will answer you, and I will tell you great and mighty things, which you do not know (Jeremiah 33:3).*

As I was praying and thinking from the other's standpoint,

I could see that they could act that way in their situations.

As I thought how heartbroken they must have been while they were observing my hopelessness, all the hatred in me melted away, and I came to love any kind of person from the depth of my heart.

Also, I kept in mind the words in the Bible telling us that there are certain things we must 'do,' 'not do,' 'keep,' and 'cast off.' I put them into practice. I wrote down each of the sinful natures that I had to cast off in a notebook, and began to cast them off through prayers and fasting. When I was assured that I had cast it off, I crossed it out with a red pen. Finally, to cross out all the sinful natures I wrote down on a notebook, it took three years.

1 John 3:9 says, *"No one who is born of God practices sin, because His seed abides in him; and he cannot sin, because he is born of God."* When we hunger and thirst for righteousness and obey and practice the word of God, this will be the evidence that we belong to God.

Eat the Flesh and Drink the Blood of the Son of Man

What is the most necessary for those who are hungry and thirsty? Of course, it is the food to fill the hunger and the drink to quench the thirst. They will be even more precious than any precious stone.

Two merchants entered a tent in a desert. They slowly began to boast of the jewels they had. One Arabian nomad who was watching them told them his story.

This nomad used to like jewels very much. While he was crossing the desert, he met with a sand-storm. He couldn't eat for several days and he was exhausted. He found a bag and opened it. It was filled with pearls, which he used to like so much.

Was he really that happy to find the pearls that he liked so much? Not really, instead he was in great despair. What he needed the most at that time was not pearls, but food and water. What is the use of pearls when you are dying of hunger?

This is the same with spirit. In John 6:55, Jesus said, *"For My flesh is true food, and My blood is true drink."* Also, He said in John 6:53, *"Truly, truly, I say to you, unless you eat the flesh of the Son of Man and drink His blood, you have no life in yourselves."*

Namely, what we need for our spirit is to gain spiritual life and enjoy the blessing of being filled by eating the flesh and drinking the blood of Jesus.

Here, the flesh of the Son of Man, Jesus, symbolizes the word of God. To eat His flesh means to take and keep in mind the word of God written in the sixty-six books of the Bible. To drink the blood of Jesus is to pray with faith and practice the word once we read, hear, and learn the word of God.

Process of the Growth of Those who Hunger and Thirst for Righteousness

1 John chapter 2 gives us a detailed description of the growth in spiritual faith and keeping eternal life by eating the flesh and drinking the blood of the Son of Man.

> *I am writing to you, little children, because your sins have been forgiven you for His name's sake. I am writing to you, fathers, because you know Him who has been from the beginning. I am writing to you, young men, because you have overcome the evil one. I have written to you, children, because you know the Father. I have written to you, fathers, because you know Him who has been from the beginning. I have written to you, young men, because you are strong, and the word of God abides in you, and you have overcome the evil one (1 John 2:12-14).*

When a man who does not know God accepts Jesus Christ and receives the forgiveness of sins, he receives the Holy Spirit and then the right to become a child of God. It means he has become like a new-born baby.

When a baby grows up and becomes a child, he comes to know the will of God more and more, as if a child recognizes his mom and dad, but he cannot really practice the word completely. It is just like children love their parents, but their thoughts are not deep and they cannot understand the heart of their parents completely.

After one passes the time as a spiritual child, he becomes a young adult in spirit who has armed himself with the word and prayer. He knows what sin is, and learns the will of God. Young adults are energetic, and they also have their own and often strong opinions. So, they are apt to make mistakes, but they have the confidence and driving force to achieve their goal.

In the young adulthood of spirit, they love God and have strong faith, so they do not take the meaningless things of the world. They are full of the Spirit, put their hope in the heavenly kingdom, and struggle against sins as they listen to the word.

They have the strength and boldness to resist trials or temptations. The word of God dwells in them, so they can overcome the enemy devil and the world and always win the victory.

As they pass the time of young adult and become like a father, they will have become mature. Through their experiences, they can think through all the aspects in the decision making process to make proper judgment in each situation. They will also gain the wisdom to lower their head from time to time.

Many people say we can understand the heart of the parents

only after we actually give birth to and raise children. Similarly, only when we become spiritual fathers can we understand the origin of God, so that we can understand His providence and possess the faith of higher level.

A father spiritually is a person who is at a level to understand the origin of God and all other secrets of the spiritual realm including the creation of the heavens and earth. Because he knows the heart and will of God, he can obey exactly according to God's heart, and therefore, he will receive love and blessings from God. He can receive all kinds of blessings including health, fame, authority, wealth, blessings of children, etc.

Blessing of Being Spiritually Satisfied

After we are born again as God's children, to the extent that we take the true food and true drink, we can grow up in spirit and go into spiritual dimension. As the depth of spiritual dimension becomes deeper, we can more easily rule over the enemy devil and Satan, and also we will be able to understand the deep heart of God the Father.

We will be able to communicate with God clearly and be guided by the Holy Spirit in all things so that we will be prosperous in all things. The life of communicating with God through the fullness of the Holy Spirit is the blessing of being satisfied given to those who hunger and thirst for righteousness.

As said in Matthew 5:6, *"Blessed are those who hunger and thirst for righteousness, for they shall be satisfied,"* those who receive the blessing of being satisfied have no reason to encounter any tests or trials.

Even if there are obstacles, God provides for us to avoid them through the guidance of the Holy Spirit. Even if we encounter difficulties, God lets us know the ways to get out of them. As our soul is prosperous, all things will go well with us, and we will be healthy; we will be guided to prosperity in all things, so that our lips will be full of testimonies.

If we are guided by the Holy Spirit like this, we will receive the strength to easily realize sins and evil and cast them off, and so, we can run towards sanctification. In the process of becoming sanctified in our Christian lives it is sometimes not easy to find things that are very deep inside our heart or very fine and small iniquities.

In this situation, if the Holy Spirit shines His light on us, we can realize what we must do and achieve. We can then go into higher levels of faith.

Also, although we do not practice the untruth to commit sins, we may not realize which way is the way that is more pleasing to God in various situations. In these cases, if we realize what it is that pleases God more by the works of the

Holy Spirit and do it, our soul will prosper even more.

Importance of True Food and True Drink

Having hundreds of thousands of dollars worth of debt, one believer was in great despair. But then, he wanted to go before God and hold on to Him. Believing he was holding on to the last hope, he began to pray and listened to the word of God with a longing heart.

He listened to the cassette tapes of sermons on his way to work and he read at least one chapter of the Bible and memorized one Bible verse every day. Then, he was reminded of the word of God in each moment of his day and he could follow it.

But it doesn't mean the gate of blessings opened immediately. As he earnestly sought God's will and prayed fervently, his faith grew. His soul was prosperous, and blessings began to come upon his business. Soon, he was able to repay the hundreds of thousands of dollars of debt he owed. His tithe today is still increasing.

Likewise, if we really hunger and thirst after righteousness, just as those who are hungry and thirsty look for food and water, we will accomplish righteousness. As a result, we will receive the blessings of health and wealth. We will receive the fullness and inspiration of the Holy Spirit and have communication with God. We will be able to accomplish the kingdom of God to the fullest degree.

'How much do I think of God, and read and meditate His word everyday?'
'How earnestly do I pray and try to practice the word of God?'

Let us check ourselves this way, and hunger and thirst for righteousness until the Lord comes back, so that we will receive the blessing of being spiritually satisfied by God the Father.
Then, we will be able to communicate with God deeply and be led in the way of a prosperous life, and more importantly, we will reach a glorious place in the heavenly kingdom.

Chapter 5
The Fifth Blessing

Blessed Are the Merciful, for They Shall Receive Mercy

Matthew 5:7

*Blessed are the merciful,
for they shall receive mercy.*

Jean Valjean in *Les Misérables* was in prison for nineteen years just for stealing a loaf of bread. After he was released, a priest provided him with food and shelter, but he stole a silver lampstand from him and ran away. He was caught and brought to the priest by the police.

The priest said he had given it to Jean Valjean to save him. By asking Jean Valjean, "Why didn't you take the saucer?" he made the detective not doubt anything.

Through this incident, Jean Valjean learned about true love and forgiveness, and began to live a new life. But detective Javert then followed Valjean and gave him hard times throughout his life. Later, Valjean saved the detective from being shot to death. He said, "There are many things that are broad such as sea, earth, and sky, but forgiveness is something broader."

Having Mercy on Others

If we forgive others with mercy, we can touch their hearts and there can be change of heart. What is the meaning of mercy?

It is the kind of heart to forgive from heart and to pray and give advice with love for somebody, even though he commits sins or directly gives hard time to us. It is similar to the goodness found in the nine fruits of the Holy Spirit in Galatians chapter 5, but it is deeper than that.

Goodness is the heart to follow only goodness without having any evil, and it is clearly seen through the heart of Jesus who did not quarrel or cry out.

> *He will not quarrel, nor cry out; nor will anyone hear His voice in the streets. A battered reed He will not break off, and a smoldering wick He will not put out, until He leads justice to victory (Matthew 12:19-20).*

Not to break off a battered reed means that even if somebody does evil, the Lord doesn't punish him immediately but bears with him until he receives salvation. For example, Jesus knew that Judas Iscariot was going to sell Him later, but He advised him with love and tried to make him understand until the end.

Also, not to put out a smoldering wick means God does not immediately forsake His children, even if they do not live by the truth. Even though we may commit sins since we are not perfect, God gives us realizations through the Holy Spirit and bears with us until the end so that we can change through the truth.

'Mercy' is to understand, forgive, and guide others to the right way with this heart of the Lord, even though they do evil to us for no reason. It is not to think from our own standpoint following our own benefit but to think from the standpoint of the others, so that we can understand others and show mercy to them.

Jesus Forgave the Adulteress

In John chapter 8, Pharisees and scribes brought a woman who was caught in the act of adultery, before Jesus. To test Him, they asked a question.

"Now in the Law Moses commanded us to stone such women; what then do You say?" (v. 5) Just imagine this situation. The woman who had committed adultery must have been shivering with the shame of her sin being revealed before everybody and the fear of death.

Those scribes and Pharisees being filled with evil intention did not take any note of the woman who was filled with fear. They were rather proud that they could now entrap Jesus. Some of the people who were watching the scene had probably picked up some rocks already in judging her according to the Law.

What did Jesus do? He quietly stooped down and with His finger wrote on the ground. It was that He wrote down the names of sins that were common for those who were present there. Then, He stood up and said, *"He who is without sin among you, let him be the first to throw a stone at her"* (v. 7).

The Jews were reminded of their sins and felt shame, and one by one they left the scene. Finally, there was only Jesus and the woman. Jesus forgave her and said, *"I do not condemn you, either. Go. From now on sin no more"* (v. 11). It must have been unforgettable for the woman for the rest of her life. She probably couldn't commit any more sins since then.

Likewise, mercy can be shown in different forms, and it can be categorized into mercy of forgiveness, mercy of punishment, and mercy of salvation.

Limitless Mercy of Salvation

Those who have accepted Jesus Christ as their Savior have already received great mercy of God. Without mercy of God, we cannot but fall into hell due to our sins and suffer forever.

But Jesus shed His blood on the cross to redeem the mankind from their sins, and when we believe it, we can be forgiven without price and can be saved: this is the mercy of God.

Even now, with the heart of the parents who nervously wait for their children who left home, God is anxiously waiting for countless souls to come forth to the way of salvation.

Also, even if somebody hurts the feelings of God so much, if he just repents with true heart and returns, God does not rebuke him saying, "Why did you disappoint Me so much? Why did you commit so many sins?" God just embraces him with His love.

> *"Come now, and let us reason together," says the LORD, "Though your sins are as scarlet, they will be as white as snow; though they are red like crimson, they will be like wool" (Isaiah 1:18).*

As far as the east is from the west, so far has He removed our transgressions from us (Psalm 103:12).

When there is somebody who had done something wrong before, if he has repented and turned back already, those who have mercy will not remember his past fault, thinking, 'He has committed such a great iniquity before.' They will not stay away from him or dislike but only forgive him. They will encourage him to help him do better.

Parable of a Servant Forgiven of Ten Thousand Talents

One day Peter asked Jesus about forgiveness. *"Lord, how often shall my brother sin against me and I forgive him? Up to seven times?"* (Matthew 18:21) Peter thought it was really generous to forgive up to seven times. Jesus answered, *"I do not say to you, up to seven times, but up to seventy times seven"* (Matthew 18:22).

This does not mean we should forgive seventy times seven, namely 490 times. Seven is a number of perfection. 'Seventy times seven' means we have to forgive limitlessly and perfectly. Then, with a parable, Jesus taught about mercy of forgiveness.

A king had many servants. One of the servants owed the king ten thousand talents, but he couldn't pay it. One talent at that time was 6,000 denarii. It is equivalent to 6,000 days' of wages. That is about sixteen years' wages of an ordinary labor.

Suppose a day's wage of an ordinary labor is 50,000 won, or about 50 US dollars. Then, one talent is so much as 300,000,000 won or approximately 300,000 US dollars. Ten thousand talents is then 3 trillion won or 3 billion US dollars. Where could a servant get this amount of money?

The king told him to sell his wife, children, and all his possessions to pay it back. The servant fell to the ground and pleaded with the king saying, *"Have patience with me and I will repay you everything"* (v. 26). The king felt compassion and released him and forgave him the debt.

This servant who had been forgiven of such a great amount of debt met with one of his fellow servants who owed him 100 denarii. A denarius was the silver coin of Roman Empire and it was one day's wage for an ordinary labor. If we suppose a day's wage as 50,000 won, the total debt this slave owed is just about 5 million won, or about 5,000 US dollars. It is really little amount compared to the ten thousand talents.

But the servant who was forgiven of his debt seized him and began to choke him, saying, 'Pay back what you owe.' Even when this man asked for mercy, he just put him in jail.

When the king came to know this fact, he was angry and said, "You wicked slave, I forgave you all that debt because you pleaded with me. Should you not also have had mercy on your fellow slave, in the same way that I had mercy on you?" and he put him in jail (Matthew 18:32-33).

It's the same with us. We who were destined to go the way of death due to sins were forgiven of our sins without any price, just with the love of Jesus Christ. But if we do not forgive little fault of others and judge and condemn them, how evil this is!

Have a Broad Heart to Forgive Others

Even if we may face some loss because of others, we should not dislike them or avoid them, but understand and embrace them. This way, we can have a broad heart to embrace many people.

If we have mercy, we don't hate anybody or have any ill-feelings against anybody. Even if the other person does something wrong in the sight of God, rather than punishing first, we should first be able to give advice out of love.

Also, when they give advice to others, some people have uncomfortable feelings about what others did and hurt their feelings giving the advice. And they should not think they are giving the advice with love. Even if they quote from the word of the truth, if they don't do it with love, they cannot receive any works of the Holy Spirit. And thus, they cannot change the heart of the others.

Even when the leaders do something wrong to their

subordinates, 1 Peter 2:18 says, *"Servants, be submissive to your masters with all respect, not only to those who are good and gentle, but also to those who are unreasonable."* Therefore, we have to obey and follow with humbleness and pray for them with love.

Also, when the subordinates do something wrong to their leaders, the leaders should not just immediately rebuke them or just leave them not to break peace for that moment. They should be able to teach with the word to let them understand correctly. This is also a kind of mercy.

When the leaders care for their subordinates with love and mercy and guide them with goodness, they can stand upright. Also, the leaders will have the sense of reward because they did the duty of guiding and managing those who are entrusted to them.

No matter what kind of situation we encounter, we should be able to understand the viewpoint of the others. We have to pray for them and give advice to them with love with which we can even give our own lives. When we have this kind of love, we may have to even punish those going wrong way as necessary to lead them to the truth.

Mercy in Punishment Containing Love

While there is mercy of forgiveness, there is also mercy of punishment. This is when the mercy is shown in the form of punishment according to the situation. This mercy of punishment is not done with any hatred or condemnation. It is originally from love.

> *For those whom the Lord loves He disciplines, and He scourges every son whom He receives. It is for discipline that you endure; God deals with you as with sons; for what son is there whom his father does not discipline? But if you are without discipline, of which all have become partakers, then you are illegitimate children and not sons (Hebrews 12:6-8).*

God loves His children, and that's why sometimes punishments are allowed to them. That way, God helps them turn from sins and act according to the truth.

Suppose your children have stolen something. Just because it is love to correct their children, there probably are not many parents who would beat their children with a switch for the first offense. If they repent with tears and from the heart, the parents will probably hug them warmly and say, "I will forgive you this time. Don't ever do it again."

But if the children say they regret and they won't do it again, but in practice they repeat the same thing, then, what should the parents do?

They should do their best to advise them. If they don't listen, although it may be heartbreaking, the parents have to use a switch and hit them also, so that they can keep it deep in their heart. Because the parents love their children, they punish them so that they can turn back before they get going into a way that is really wrong.

When Children Commit Sins

A thief who was standing in the court asked the authorities to let him see his mother before the trial. When he met his mother, he cried out saying it was all her fault that he became a thief. He said that he became a thief because his mother did not punish him when he first stole something in his childhood.

When asked why they do not punish their children who do something wrong, most parents would say that it is because they love their children. But Proverbs 13:24 says, *"He who withholds his rod hates his son, but he who loves him disciplines him diligently."*

If we just think of our children, 'Oh, my dear baby,' then, even the wrongdoings that they do seem to be lovely. Because of this kind of fleshly affection, many people do not discern between what is right and wrong, and make wrong judgments.

Also, even when the children continually act inappropriately, the parents do not correct them, but just accept it. Then, the behavior of the children becomes increasingly misdirected and misguided.

For example, in 1 Samuel chapter 2, we see the priest Eli's two sons, Hophni and Phinehas lay with the women who served at the doorway of the tent of meeting. But Eli just told them, *"No, my sons; for the report is not good which I hear the LORD's people circulating"* (v. 24). The two sons kept on sinning and faced a miserable death.

If the priest Eli had admonished them sternly and sometimes rebuked them as necessary to go the proper way of a priest, they wouldn't have gone the wrong way to that extent. They reached a point where they could not turn back because their father did not raise them properly in the right way.

But even in the same kind of punishment, if it has no love in it, we cannot say it is mercy. Suppose a child of one of your neighbors stole something from you. Then, what would you do?

Those who have goodness will have mercy on him and forgive him if the child is asking for forgiveness from heart. But those who do not have goodness will get angry at the child and scold him, or even if he asks for forgiveness, they will still demand punishment. Or, they may reveal this and spread it to many people, or remember it for a long time and develop prejudice against the child.

This kind of punishment comes from hatred, and thus it is not mercy. It cannot change the other person. When we punish, we have to punish that person with love considering his standpoint and his future to make it punishment in mercy.

When Brothers in Faith Sin

When a brother in faith sins, the Bible tells us in detail how to deal with him.

If your brother sins, go and show him his fault in private; if he listens to you, you have won your brother. But if he does not listen to you, take one or two more with you, so that by the mouth of two or three witnesses every fact may be confirmed. If he refuses to listen to them, tell it to the church; and if he refuses to listen even to the church, let him be to you as a Gentile and a tax collector (Matthew 18:15-17).

When we see a brother in faith sins, we should not spread it to others. First, we have to talk to him personally so that he can turn away. If he doesn't listen, we should talk together with those who are higher in his group so that he can turn away.

If he still doesn't listen, we have to tell the church authorities to lead him to the way of salvation. If he still doesn't listen to the church authorities, then, the Bible tells us to regard him as an unbeliever. We should not judge or condemn even a person who commits a grave sin. Only when we show love and mercy can we receive mercy from God, too.

Mercy in Charitable Works

It is something obvious for God's children to take care of those who are in need and show mercy to them. When brothers in faith suffer, if we just say we are sorry but show no deeds, then, we cannot be said to have mercy. The mercy in charitable works in God's sight is to share what we have with brothers who are in need.

James 2:15-16 says, *"If a brother or sister is without clothing and in need of daily food, and one of you says to them, 'Go in peace, be warmed and be filled,' and yet you do not give them what is necessary for their body, what use is that?"*

Some may say, "I really want to help, but I don't have anything to give to help them." But which parents would just watch their children starving, just because they are in a financial difficulty? In the same way, we should be able to act towards our brothers in a way we would do to our own children.

Those Who Are Punished Due to Their Sins

When we show mercy and help the needy, we have to keep something in mind. It is the fact that we should not help those who are in difficulties because of their sins against God. This is to cause problems to come upon ourselves.

During the reign of King Jeroboam in the kingdom of Israel, there was a prophet called Jonah. In the book of Jonah, we see people who fell into a difficult situation together with the prophet Jonah who disobeyed God.

One day God told Jonah to go to the city of Nineveh, which was the capital city of a country that was hostile to Israel, and proclaim the warning of God. It was that the city of Nineveh was filled with sins and God would destroy it.

Jonah knew that, if the people in the Nineveh repented after hearing the warning of God, they would escape the destruction. He knew the heart of God who has limitless mercy and is love itself. Then, it was like helping Assyria, which was hostile to Israel. So, Jonah disobeyed the word of God and got onboard a ship going to Tarshish.

So, God sent a big storm, and the people on the ship threw out all they had onboard and took a great loss. They finally came to know that it was because of Jonah who disobeyed God. They knew that the storm would stop if they threw Jonah out to the sea as Jonah told them, but with their sympathy for him they couldn't do it. They had to suffer with him until they threw him off board.

Taking this example as a lesson, when we show our mercy, we have to be wise. We have to understand that if we help those who are in difficulties because of God's punishment, we will fall into the same kind of difficulties.

Also, in a different case, if somebody is healthy but not working just because he is lazy, it is not right to help such a person. It is the same with those who habitually ask other people for help, although they can also work.

To help these people is to make them lazier and less capable. If we show mercy that is not right in the sight of God, it will block the blessings on us.

Thus, we should not just unconditionally help everybody who is in difficulties. We should discern each case so that we will not face difficulties ourselves after helping others.

Show Mercy to Unbelievers

Here, one important thing is that we should show our mercy not only to brothers in faith but also to unbelievers.

Most people want to have friendships with others who have wealth and fame, but they look down on and do not want to be close to those who failed in their walks in life. They may help such people a couple of times because of previous friendships, but it will not go on. But we should not look down on or despise anybody. We have to consider others better than us and treat everybody with love.

There are some who really have merciful hearts that have regard for the difficulties of other people. There are some people who reluctantly help others because of the eyes of other people. God looks at the inner heart of men. He says that mercy is to help with true love, and He will bless those who show true mercy.

Blessings on Those who are Merciful

What are the blessings of God given to those who are merciful? Matthew 5:7 says, *"Blessed are the merciful, for they shall receive mercy."*

If we can forgive and show mercy even to those who give us hard times and cause us to suffer damages, God will show mercy on us and give us chances to be forgiven even when we cause damage to occur to others by mistake.

The Lord's Prayer says, *"And forgive us our debts, as we also have forgiven our debtors"* (Matthew 6:12). We open the way to receive mercy from God by showing mercy to others.

At the time of early church, there was a disciple named Tabitha (Acts 9:36-42). The believers in Jerusalem spread out to many places because of severe persecutions. Some of them settled down in a port city called Joppa. This city became one of the centers for Christians, where Tabitha was living.

She helped those who were poor and in need. But one day she became sick and died.

Those who had received help from her sent people to Peter to ask him to revive her. They showed all the tunics and garments that she used to make while she was with them, taking about all the good things she had done.

Finally, she experienced the amazing work of God being raised to life again through the prayer of Peter. She received the blessing of her life being extended by the mercy of God.

Also, when we have mercy on those who are poor and sick, God gives us the blessing of being healthy and wealthy.

Because of poverty and diseases of which I couldn't see the end, I had to spend difficult times in my youth. Through that time though, I came to understand the heart of those who experience difficulties.

For more than thirty years from the time I was healed of all my diseases by the power of God, I have been living disease-free without any kind of sickness. Yet, I cannot lose the loving sympathy I have towards those who are suffering from illnesses and poverty, and those who are neglected and forsaken.

So, not only before I opened this church, but also after the opening of the church I wanted to give a hand to those who were in need. I didn't think, "I will help when I become rich." I just helped others whether it was big or small amount.

God was pleased with this deed, and He blessed me so much that I can abundantly offer to God for world mission and for accomplishing God's kingdom. As I sowed the seed of mercy for others, God let me reap an abundant harvest.

If we show mercy to others, God will also forgive our iniquities. He will fill us so that we lack nothing, and He'll change weaknesses into health. This is the mercy that we can receive from God when we are merciful to others.

John 13:34 says, *"A new commandment I give to you, that you love one another, even as I have loved you, that you also love one another."* As said, let us give comfort and life to many people with the aroma of mercy, so that we will enjoy abundant life in the blessings of God.

Chapter 6
The Sixth Blessing

Blessed Are the Pure in Heart, for They Shall See God

Matthew 5:8

Blessed are the pure in heart,
for they shall see God.

"The first thing I felt when I landed on the moon is the creation of God and the glorious presence of God."

It is the proclamation made by James Irwin, who went to the moon on the Apollo 15, in 1971. This was a very famous quote that touched many people around the globe. When he was giving a lecture in Hungary, one student asked him.

"None of the astronauts of Soviet Union said they saw God in the universe, but why do you say you saw God in the universe and praised His glory?"

The Irwin's answer was so clear to everyone that it was indisputable. "Those who are pure in heart can see God!" He stayed on the moon for 18 hours, and it is said that he recited Psalm 8 seeing the earth and the universe that God created.

> "O LORD, our LORD,
> How majestic is Your name in all the earth,
> Who have displayed
> Your splendor above the heavens! ...
> When I consider Your heavens,
> the work of Your fingers,
> The moon and the stars,
> which You have ordained...
> O LORD, our LORD,
> How majestic is Your name in all the earth!"

The Pure in Heart before God

The Merriam-Webster's Online Dictionary defines 'pure' as 'unmixed with any other matter, or free from dust, dirt, or other contaminant.' In the Bible, it means we have to act in a holy manner not only on the outside with knowledge and education, but we also have to have a holy and sanctified heart.

In Matthew 15, when Jesus was ministering in Galilee, scribes and Pharisees came from Jerusalem.

The scribes and Pharisees were the ones who professionally taught the Law to the people, and they kept the Law very strictly. They also kept the traditions of the elders, which were detailed regulations on how to keep the Law. These traditions have been passed down throughout generations.

Because they practiced a great deal of self-control and lived ascetic lives, they thought they were holy. But their hearts were filled with evil. When they were offended by the word of Jesus, they tried to kill Him.

One of the traditions of the elders made by the scribes and Pharisees said that it was not clean to eat with unwashed hands.

And they saw the disciples of Jesus eating with unwashed hands, and in objection to this they asked Jesus a question.

They asked Jesus, *"Why do Your disciples break the tradition of the elders?"* (v. 2) Then, Jesus said, *"It is not what enters into the mouth that defiles the man, but what proceeds out of the mouth, this defiles the man"* (v. 11).

> *But the things that proceed out of the mouth come from the heart, and those defile the man. For out of the heart come evil thoughts, murders, adulteries, fornications, thefts, false witness, and slanders. These are the things which defile the man; but to eat with unwashed hands does not defile the man (Matthew 15:18-20).*

Jesus also rebuked them saying they were whitewashed tombs (Matthew 23:27). In Israel they usually used a cave as a tomb. Usually they painted the entrance of the tomb with white lime.

But a tomb is a place for a corpse, and no matter how much we decorate it, the inside is still full of decay and it is foul smelling. Jesus likened the scribes and Pharisees to the whitewashed tombs because they were acting holy on the outside but their heart was filled with various evils and sins.

God wants us to be beautiful not only on the outside but also within the heart. That is why He said, *"For God sees not as man sees, for man looks at the outward appearance, but the LORD looks at the heart"* (1 Samuel 16:7) when He anointed David, a shepherd, as the king of Israel.

How Pure Am I in Heart?

When we preach the gospel, some people say, "I did not harm anybody and lived a good life, so I can go to heaven." They mean that they can go to heaven even if they do not believe in Jesus Christ because they have good hearts and did not commit sins.

But Romans 3:10 says, *"As it is written, 'There is none righteous, not even one.'"* No matter how righteous and good one thinks of himself, he will realize that he has so many iniquities and sins if he reflects himself upon the word of God. But some say that they don't have any sin because they did not harm anybody and did not break the law.

For example, even though they hate somebody, they think they are sinless because they did not cause any physical harm to the person. But God says that having evil in heart is also a sin.

He says in 1 John 3:15, *"Everyone who hates his brother is a murderer; and you know that no murderer has eternal life abiding in him,"* and in Matthew 5:28, *"But I say to you that everyone who looks at a woman with lust for her has already committed adultery with her in his heart."*

Even though it is not seen in action, if one has hatred, an adulterous mind, selfish desires, arrogance, falsehood, jealousy, and anger in his heart, his heart is not pure. Those who are pure in heart will not put their interest in meaningless things but strictly follow just the one way with an unchanging heart.

Deeds of Ruth, a Woman with a Pure Heart

Ruth was a Gentile woman who became a widow at a young age without having any children. She would not abandon her mother-in-law, but stayed with her even in bad times. Her mother-in-law had nobody to rely on, yet for Ruth's sake she told Ruth to go back to her own family. But Ruth could not leave her mother-in-law alone.

> But Ruth said, "Do not urge me to leave you or turn back from following you; for where you go, I will go, and where you lodge, I will lodge. Your people shall be my people, and your God, my God. Where you die, I will die, and there I will be buried. Thus may the LORD do to me, and worse, if anything but death parts you and me" (Ruth 1:16-17).

This confession of Ruth contains her strong will and love with all her life in service to her mother-in-law. Her mother-in-law's hometown was in Israel, a place unfamiliar to Ruth. They didn't have a house or anything there.

But she did not think of those circumstances, but only chose to serve her mother-in-law who was alone. Ruth never regretted her choice and just served her mother-in-law with an unchanging heart.

Because Ruth had such a pure heart, she could sacrifice herself with joy and unchangingly served her mother-in-law. As a result, she met a rich man named Boaz who was also a good man according to the customs of Israel, and they had a happy family. She became the great grandmother of the King David and her name was even entered into the genealogy of Jesus.

Blessings for the Pure in Heart

What kinds of blessings will the pure in heart receive? Matthew 5:8 says, *"Blessed are the pure in heart, for they shall see God."*

It's always something joyful to be with those who are dear to us. God is the Father of our spirit, and He loves us more than ourselves. If we can see Him face to face and be at His side, that happiness cannot be compared with anything else.

Some may ask, "How can a man see God?" Judges 13:22 says, *"So Manoah said to his wife, "We will surely die, for we have seen God."*

John 1:18 says, *"No one has seen God at any time."* In many places in the Bible, we can find that people were not supposed to be able to see God and if they did, they would die.

But, Exodus 33:11 says, *"Thus the LORD used to speak to Moses face to face, just as a man speaks to his friend."* When the Israelites reached the Mount Sinai after the Exodus, God came down, and they could not approach in fear of dying, but Moses could see God (Exodus 20:18-19).

Furthermore, Genesis 5:21-24 tells us that Enoch walked

with God.

> *Enoch lived sixty-five years, and became the father of Methuselah. Then Enoch walked with God three hundred years after he became the father of Methuselah, and he had other sons and daughters. So all the days of Enoch were three hundred and sixty-five years. Enoch walked with God; and he was not, for God took him.*

To walk with God does not mean God Himself came down to earth and walked with Enoch. It means Enoch always communicated with God and God took control of everything in Enoch's life.

One thing we have to know here is that 'walking together' and 'being together' are completely different from each other. 'God being together' means He keeps us with His angels.

When we try to live by the word, God protects us, but He can walk with us only after we become completely sanctified. Therefore, by seeing the fact that Enoch walked with God for three hundred years, we can see how much he was loved by God.

Blessing of Seeing God

Then, what is the reason that some men cannot see God

whereas some others see God face to face and even walk with Him?

3 John 1:11 says, *"Beloved, do not imitate what is evil, but what is good. The one who does good is of God; the one who does evil has not seen God."* As said, those who are pure in heart can see God, but those whose hearts are unclean with evil cannot see God.

We can see it from the case of Stephen who became a martyr while preaching the gospel at the time of early church. In Acts chapter 7, we can see that Stephen had been preaching the gospel of Jesus Christ and was praying even for those who were stoning him. It means that to that extent he was pure and didn't have sins in heart. That's why he could see the Lord who was standing at the right hand of God.

Those who can see God are pure in heart, and they can go into the better dwelling places in heaven in the third kingdom of heaven or higher. They can see the Lord and God closely and enjoy happiness forever.

But those who go into the First Kingdom or the Second Kingdom of Heaven cannot see the Lord closely even if they want to because the spiritual lights that radiate in them and the dwelling places are different according to the level of sanctification.

How to Become Pure in Heart

The holy and perfect God wants us to be perfect and pure not only in the deeds but also in the heart by casting off sins that are placed deep inside our heart. That is why He says, *"You shall be holy, for I am holy"* (1 Peter 1:16), and *"For this is the will of God, your sanctification; that is, that you abstain from sexual immorality"* (1 Thessalonians 4:3).

Now, what do we have to do to have pure heart that God requires of us and accomplish holiness in us?

Those who used to get angry have to cast off the anger and become gentle. Those who used to be arrogant must cast off arrogance and humble themselves. Those who used to hate others must change to be able to love even their enemies. Simply put, we have to cast off all forms of evil and struggle against sins to the point of shedding blood (Hebrews 12:4).

To the extent that we cast off evil from our heart, listen to God's word, practice it, and fill ourselves with the truth, we can have pure hearts. It will be pointless if we just hear the word and not practice it. Suppose the clothes are dirty, and we just say, "Oh, I have to wash it," but just leave them lie.

Therefore, if we realize the filthy things in our heart by listening to the word of God, we have to try hard to cast them off. Of course, the purity in heart cannot be achieved merely with men's strength and willpower. We can understand this through the confession of the apostle Paul.

> *For I joyfully concur with the law of God in the inner man, but I see a different law in the members of my body, waging war against the law of my mind and making me a prisoner of the law of sin which is in my members. Wretched man that I am! Who will set me free from the body of this death? (Romans 7:22-24)*

Here, the 'inner man' refers to the original heart given by God, which is the heart of truth, rejoicing in the law of God and seeking God. On the other hand, there is the heart of untruth that desires to commit sins, so we cannot cast off sins just with our effort alone.

For example, we can see this in people who cannot easily quit drinking and smoking. They know cigarette smoking and excessive alcohol is harmful, but they cannot quit. They make New Year's resolutions and try to quit, but they can't.

They know it's harmful, but because they actually like it, they cannot quit. But, if they receive God's strength from above, they can quit at once.

It's the same with the sins and evil in our heart. 1 Timothy 4:5 says, *"For it is sanctified by means of the word of God and prayer."* As said, when we realize the truth through the word of God, and receive God's grace, strength, and the help of the Holy Spirit through fervent prayer, we can cast them off.

To do this, what we need is our effort and willpower to practice the word of God. We should not just stop after practicing the word a couple of times. If we pray and sometimes fast until we finally change, then we can really cast off all sins and have pure hearts.

The Pure in Heart Receive Answers and Blessings

The blessings of those who are pure in heart are not just to see the image of the Father God. It means they can receive the answers to their desires of the heart through prayers, and they can meet and experience God in their lives.

Jeremiah 29:12-13 says, *"Then you will call upon Me and come and pray to Me, and I will listen to you. You will seek Me and find Me when you search for Me with all your heart."* They will receive the answers of God through their earnest prayers, so that they will have many testimonies in their lives.

But sometimes, we see some new-believers who have just accepted Jesus Christ, and do not really live in the truth, but receive answers to their prayers. Even though their hearts are not completely pure, they are meeting and experiencing the living God.

This is like a case where little children do something very lovely and the parents give them what they want. Even though they have not accomplished pure hearts completely, to the extent that they please God within the measure of their faith, they can receive the answers to their various prayers.

After I met God, was healed of all my diseases, and recovered my health, I was looking for a job. But even if they offered me very good conditions, I did not take any of those offers if I could not keep the Lord's Day holy because of the work. I tried my best to follow the right way with a pure heart before God.

God was pleased with this kind of heart and guided me to run a small book rental shop. It was going well, and I was planning to move to a bigger place. I heard there was one suitable place.

When I went there, the shop owner there did not want to sign the contract with me because his business was not good because my shop was going well. I had to give up, but when I thought from his viewpoint, I was sorry for him, and I prayed for his blessings from the bottom of my heart.

Later, I came to know that, one big book shop would open right in front of that shop. In that shop I wouldn't have been competition for such a big shop. God who knows everything worked for the good of everything and prevented that contract from being made.

Later, I moved into a different shop. I did not accept any disorderly students. Smoking cigarettes and drinking liquor was prohibited in my shop. On Sunday, when there was the most number of customers, I closed the door to keep the Lord's Day. In human thought, the business could not be good in any way. But rather, the number of the customers increased and the sales increased. So everybody had to recognize that it was the blessing of God.

By the way, as we lead a Christian life, we can also receive the gift of speaking in another tongue or other gifts of the Holy Spirit. This is partly the blessing of "seeing God."

> *To another faith by the same Spirit, and to another gifts of healing by the one Spirit, and to another the effecting of miracles, and to another prophecy, and to another the distinguishing of spirits, to another various kinds of tongues, and to another the interpretation of tongues. But one and the same Spirit works all these things, distributing to each one individually just as He wills (1 Corinthians 12:9-11).*

What we have to remember is that if we truly love God, then we should not be satisfied with the faith of a child. We have to try our best to cast off all evils from our heart and become quickly sanctified so that we will mature faith and understand the heart of God.

2 Corinthians 7:1 says, *"Therefore, having these promises, beloved, let us cleanse ourselves from all defilement of flesh and spirit, perfecting holiness in the fear of God."* As said, let us cast off all defilement of heart and accomplish holiness in us.

I hope that we will be prosperous in all things and receive whatever we ask, just as a tree planted by the water will not dry, but bear abundant fruits even in drought. I also hope that we will all be able to see God face to face in the eternal heavenly kingdom.

Chapter 7
The Seventh Blessing

Blessed Are the Peacemakers, for They Shall Be Called Sons of God

Matthew 5:9

*Blessed are the peacemakers,
for they shall be called sons of God.*

When there are two countries that share a border, they may have conflicts or even wars each fighting to gain their own benefit or advantage. But there are two countries that share the same border, but they have had peace for a long time. They are Argentina and Chile.

Long ago, they had a crisis that almost got them into a war because of the conflicts along the border. The religious leaders of both countries pleaded with the people saying that love was the only way to keep peace between the two countries. The people accepted what they were told and chose peace. They erected a post with the Bible verse from Ephesians 2:14, *"For He Himself is our peace, who made both groups into one and broke down the barrier of the dividing wall."*

To have peace between countries is to have a good relationship between them, and in personal relationships they must have comfortable hearts between one another. However the spiritual meaning of peace with God is a little different. It is to sacrifice ourselves for others and serve them. It is to humble ourselves to lift up others. We don't behave rudely. Even when we are right, we can follow the other person's opinions unless they are untruth.

It is to seek everyone's benefit. It is not insisting on our personal opinions, but considering others first. It is to follow others' opinions and to have no partiality and to be mutually compatible with both sides of a problem or given situation. To be a peacemaker, we need to sacrifice ourselves. Therefore, the spiritual meaning of peace is to sacrifice ourselves even to give our lives.

Jesus Made Peace by Sacrificing Himself

When God created the first man Adam, he was a living spirit. He enjoyed the authority of ruling over everything. But, as sin came into him by eating the forbidden fruit, Adam and all his descendants became sinners. Now there was a wall of sin between men and God.

As said in Colossians 1:21, *"You were formerly alienated and hostile in mind, engaged in evil deeds,"* men were alienated from God because of sins.

Mankind had become sinners from the time of Adam, and Jesus, the Son of God, became the atoning sacrifice for us. He died on the cross to destroy the wall of sin between God and men and made peace.

One may ask, "Why did all mankind have to become sinners just because of the sin of Adam since he was just one person?" It's somewhat like long time ago when there were slaves. Once you become a slave, all your descendants were born as slaves.

Romans 6:16 says, *"Do you not know that when you present yourselves to someone as slaves for obedience, you are slaves of the one whom you obey, either of sin resulting in death, or of obedience resulting in righteousness?"* Because Adam obeyed the enemy devil and committed sin, everyone after him became a sinner.

To bring peace between God and mankind who became sinners, sinless Jesus was crucified. Colossians 1:20 says, *"And through Him to reconcile all things to Himself, having made peace through the blood of His cross; through Him, I say whether things on earth or things in heaven."* Jesus became the atoning sacrifice for the forgiveness of our sins and He brought peace between God and men.

Are You a Peacemaker?

Just as Jesus came down to this earth in human flesh and became the Peacemaker, God wants us to have peace with everyone. Of course, when we believe in God and learn the truth, usually we will not intentionally break peace. But as long as we have our own righteousness thinking that we are right, we may unknowingly break peace.

We can realize whether we are this kind of person by checking whether we are making everything fitting others or others are trying to make everything fitting us. For example, between a husband and a wife, suppose the wife doesn't like salty food while the husband likes salty food.

The wife is telling her husband that salty food is not good for health, but he still likes salty food. So, the wife doesn't understand him. From the standpoint of the husband, he cannot easily change his taste.

Here, if the wife is insisting that her husband follow her advice because she is right, quarrels may arise. Therefore, to have peace, we should consider others and help them understand to make changes little by little for the better.

Likewise, when we look around, we can easily see that the peace breaks because of such little things. It's because of our own righteousness thinking that we are right.

Therefore, we should check ourselves as to whether we are seeking our own benefit before others' benefit, or whether we are trying to insist on our opinions because we are right and we are speaking the truth, although we know the other person is having a hard time. Also, we should check whether we want our subordinates to unconditionally obey and follow us just because we are the seniors.

Then, we can realize whether we are really peacemakers. Generally, it is easy to have peace with those who are nice to us. But God tells us to have peace with all men and sanctification.

> *Pursue peace with all men, and the sanctification without which no one will see the Lord (Hebrews 12:14).*

We should be able to have peace even with those who dislike us, hate us, or cause us difficulties. Even though it seems that we are absolutely right, if the other person is having a hard time or is uncomfortable because of us, it is not right in the sight of God. Then, how can we have peace with all men?

Have Peace with God

First, we have to have peace with God.

Isaiah 59:1-2 says, *"Behold, the LORD's hand is not so short that it cannot save; nor is His ear so dull that it cannot hear. But your iniquities have made a separation between you and your God, and your sins have hidden His face from you so that He does not hear."* If we commit sins, a wall of sin will block us from God.

Therefore, to have peace with God is having no wall of sin resulting from sins between God and us.

When we accept Jesus Christ, we are forgiven of all sins that we have committed until then (Ephesians 1:7). Because of this, the wall of sin between God and us is destroyed, and peace is established.

But we have to keep in mind that if we keep on committing sins after our sins are forgiven, the wall of sin is created again.

We can understand from the Bible that many kinds of problems are caused by sin. When Jesus healed a paralytic man in Matthew chapter 9, He first forgave his sin. After He healed a man who had been sick for 38 years, He said, in John 5:14,

"Behold, you have become well; do not sin anymore, so that nothing worse happens to you."

Therefore, when we repent our sins, turn back and live by the word of God, we can have peace with God. Then we can also receive blessings as His children. If we have a disease, we will be healed and made healthy, if we have financial difficulties, the problem will go away and we will be rich. In this way, we receive answers to our hearts' desires.

Have Peace with Yourself

As long as we have hatred, envy, jealousy and other kinds of evil, they will be agitated according to the situation. Then, we will suffer because of them and we cannot have peace.

There is a Korean saying that goes, "When your cousin buys land, you get a stomachache." This is expression of envy. One will suffer because of envy, not liking the situation where others are well-off. Likewise, as long as we have envy, jealousy, arrogance, quarreling, adulterous mind, and other forms of evil in our heart, we cannot have peace. The Holy Spirit in us will also groan, so our heart will feel distressed.

Therefore, to have peace with ourselves, we have to cast off evil from our heart and follow the desires of the Holy Spirit.

When we accept Jesus Christ and have peace with God, God sends the gift of the Holy Spirit into our heart (Acts 2:38).

The Holy Spirit, the heart of God, lets us call God "Father." He lets us realize about sin, righteousness, and judgment. God's children can then live by the word of God being guided by the Holy Spirit.

When we practice the word of God and follow the desires of the Holy Spirit with this help of the Holy Spirit, He rejoices in our heart. So, we can have comfort in heart, and we can have peace with ourselves.

Furthermore, to the extent that we completely cast off evil from our heart, we don't have any more struggles against sins, so we can have complete peace with ourselves. Only after we have peace with ourselves can we have peace with others, too.

Have Peace among Men

Sometimes, we can see people who have fervor and passion for their God-given duties. They love God and devote themselves, but they have no peace with other brothers in faith.

If they think that it is beneficial for the kingdom of God, they don't listen to others' opinions but just continue to passionately progress on their work. Then, some others will become uncomfortable and have feelings of opposition towards them.

In this situation, the ones who do not have peace with others will think that it is the price they have to pay for in order to accomplish something good for the kingdom of God. They don't really care even if there are some people who have opinions opposite of their own or they have caused uncomfortable feelings to arise in others.

But those with goodness will consider the heart of everybody concerned, so that they can follow peace and embrace others. So, many people can come to them.

Goodness is the heart of truth that follows goodness in truth. It is to be nice and generous. Also, it is to consider others better than ourselves and care for others (Philippians 2:3-5).

Matthew 12:19-20 says, *"He will not quarrel, nor cry out; Nor will anyone hear His voice in the streets. A battered reed He will not break off, and a smoldering wick He will not put out, until He leads justice to victory."*

If we have this kind of goodness, we will not quarrel with others. We will not try to boast or be lifted up. We will love even those who are as weak as a battered reed or as evil as a smoldering wick. We will embrace them hoping the best for them.

For example, suppose the first son is buying very good presents for his parents out of his love for them. But if he criticizes his brothers who cannot do the same, how will his parents feel about it? Probably, they would want their children to have peace and love rather than receiving expensive and good presents.

In the same way, God wants us to understand His heart and resemble His heart first rather than accomplishing His kingdom greatly. Unless it is absolute untruth, we should be considerate of the weak faith of others to follow peace.

Since pasturing this church, I have never had any uncomfortable feelings against those pastors or workers who did not yield proper fruits. I looked at them with faith and with perseverance until they received more strength from God and fulfilled their duties well.

If I just insist on my standpoint, I might have advised them saying something like, "Why don't you do another job, receive more power next year, and then you can get back to this job later."

But with fear that some would lose heart, I didn't do that. When we have goodness not to break the battered reed or snuff out a smoldering wick, we can have peace with all men.

Peace through Our Sacrifice

John 12:24 says, *"Truly, truly, I say to you, unless a grain of wheat falls into the earth and dies, it remains alone; but if it dies, it bears much fruit."* As said, when we sacrifice ourselves completely in each area, we can have peace and abundant fruit. Namely, when the seed falls to the ground and dies, it can sprout and bear much fruit.

What did Jesus do? He sacrificed Himself completely. He was crucified for mankind who are all sinners. He opened the way of salvation and regained untold numbers of God's children.

Likewise, when we sacrifice first, when we serve others in

each area whether it is in the family, workplace, or church, then we can have the beautiful fruit of peace.

Everyone has different measures of faith (Romans 12:3). Each one has different opinions and ideas. The level of education, the characters, and the circumstances in which they were raised are all different, so everyone has different standards on what he likes and what he thinks is right.

Everybody has a different standard, and so, if each one insists upon what he wants, we can never have peace. Even if we are right, and even if we may have some discomfort because of others, we have to sacrifice ourselves to have peace.

Suppose two sisters who have completely different life styles are sharing a room.

The older one likes things to be clean, but the younger one is not really like that. The older one asks her younger one to change. When the younger sister doesn't listen a couple of times, the older sister may get irritated. She will finally show it on the outside, too. Eventually, there will be a quarrel.

Here, obviously to have a clean room is better, but if we get angry and offend others with our words, it is not right. Even if we may have something uncomfortable, we should wait with love for that person until he changes to have peace.

There was a man called Minson. He lost his mother when he was very young. He had a stepmother. His stepmother had two younger sons.

She mistreated Minson; she gave good food and good clothes only to her own sons. Minson had to shiver in cold winter wearing clothes made of reeds.

On a cold winter day, while Minson was pushing the cart that his father was pulling, he shivered so much that the shivering was passed on to the cart. His father touched his son's clothes and finally realized his son was wearing clothes of reeds.

"How can she do this?" He was enraged, and he was about to kick his new wife out of the house. But then Minson pleaded with his father not to do that. "Father, please don't be upset. When their mother is here, only one son will suffer, but if she is kicked out, all three sons will suffer."

The stepmother was touched by what he said. She repented her wrongdoings with tears and they had a peaceful family after that.

Likewise, those who have meekness like cotton and have no quarrels or troubles with others will be welcomed and loved everywhere. Such people are peacemakers. They can sacrifice themselves for others even giving their lives.

Abraham the Peacemaker

Most people want to have peace in their lives, but they cannot really do that. It's because they seek their own benefits and advantages.

If we don't seek for ourselves, it may seem that we will face loss, but with the eyes of faith, it's not true. When we follow the will of God to seek the benefit of others, God will repay us with His answers and blessings.

In Genesis chapter 13, we see Abraham and his nephew Lot. Lot had lost his father early in his life and followed Abraham like his own father. As a result, he also received blessings when Abraham was loved and blessed by God. Their possessions were substantial. Not only silver and gold, but they also had many cattle. So, the water was not enough, and the shepherds from the two sides had quarrels.

Finally, to prevent quarrels between the families, Abraham decided to separate the dwelling place. At this time, Abraham gave the right of first choice to choose the better land.

> *Is not the whole land before you? Please separate from me; if to the left, then I will go to the right; or if to the right, then I will go to the left (Genesis 13:9).*

So, Lot took the valley of Jordan for it had plenty of water. From the standpoint of Abraham, Lot was blessed because of him, and in the order of the family, he was the uncle and Lot was the nephew, so he could have taken the better land first. Also, if Abraham had given the right of first choice to Lot as a mere action, he would have thought it was improper act from

Lot.

But, from the bottom of his heart, Abraham wanted his nephew Lot to take the better land. That's why he could have peace with Lot, and as a result, he received even greater blessings from God.

> *The LORD said to Abram, after Lot had separated from him, "Now lift up your eyes and look from the place where you are, northward and southward and eastward and westward; for all the land which you see, I will give it to you and to your descendants forever. I will make your descendants as the dust of the earth, so that if anyone can number the dust of the earth, then your descendants can also be numbered. Arise, walk about the land through its length and breadth; for I will give it to you" (Genesis 13:14-17).*

Since then, Abraham's wealth and authority were so great that he was respected even by the kings around him. With his good heart, he could even be called a 'friend of God.'

He who seeks others' benefit in all things will do the things that others want, not what he wants. If he is struck on the right cheek, he will turn his left cheek. He can give his cloak as well as his tunic to someone who asks him for this, and he can go two miles with those who force him to go one mile with him

(Matthew 5:39-41).

Just as Jesus also prayed for those who were crucifying Him, he can also pray for his enemies and for their blessings. He can pray for those who persecute him. When we sacrifice ourselves from the depth of our heart and seek others' benefit, we can have peace.

Peace in Truth Only

One thing we have to be careful about is that there is a difference between being patient and covering others' faults to have peace and just ignoring something disparagingly. Having peace doesn't mean we just avoid or compromise with a person when a brother is sinning. We have to have peace with everybody but we have to have peace within the truth.

For example, we may be asked to bow down before idols by family members or colleagues in the work place. They may ask us to drink alcohol. This is against the word of God (Exodus 20:4-5; Ephesians 5:18), so we have to refuse it and choose the way that is pleasing to God.

But when we do that, we have to be wise. We should not hurt the others' feelings. We have to be kind to them all the time. We have to gain their heart with our faithfulness. We can then persuade them with a gentle heart and ask for their understanding.

This is a testimony of one of the sisters in our church. After she was employed, she had some troubles with her colleagues for some time. They wanted her to come to the outings and other meetings on Sundays, but she wanted to keep the Lord's Day holy.

So, her colleagues and seniors left her out intentionally. But she didn't care about it and just kept on working faithfully, even voluntarily doing errands of other employees. When they saw her giving out this kind of fragrance of the Christ, they were touched by her. Now, they have meetings on other days than Sunday, and they even set their wedding days on Saturdays, not on Sunday.

The Blessing of Being Called Sons of God

Matthew 5:9 says, *"Blessed are the peacemakers, for they shall be called sons of God."* How great blessing is it to be called a son of God?

Here 'sons' does not only refer to only males, but all children of God. But it is a little different from the 'sons' in Galatians 3:26 which says, *"For you are all sons of God through faith in Christ Jesus."* In Galatians it is just the sons who are saved. But the 'sons of God' for peacemakers have deeper spiritual meaning. Namely, it is the true children whom God Himself acknowledges.

All who have accepted Jesus Christ and have faith are children of God. John 1:12 says, *"But as many as received Him, to them He gave the right to become children of God, even to those who believe in His name."* But even though we have all been saved and become God's children, not every believer is the same.

For example, among many children, there are some who understand the hearts of the parents and give comfort, while others are only giving hard times to their parents.

Likewise, even from the viewpoint of God, some children quickly cast off evil from their heart and obey the word, while other children are not changing even after a long period of time. They just keep on disobeying.

Here, which children would God consider better? Obviously it is those who resemble the Lord, have pure hearts, and obey the word. So, Genesis 17:1 says, *"I am God Almighty; walk before Me, and be blameless."* God wants His children to be blameless and perfect.

In order for us to be called sons of God, we have to resemble the image of Jesus our Savior (Romans 8:29). Jesus, the Son of God, became the peacemaker by sacrificing Himself even unto His crucifixion.

Likewise, when we resemble Jesus in sacrificing ourselves and pursue peace we can be called sons of God. We can then also enjoy the spiritual authority and power that Jesus enjoyed (Matthew 10:1).

Just as Jesus healed many diseases, drove out demons, and revived the dead, if we are called sons of God then we can also heal even incurable diseases such as cancer, AIDS, and leukemia.

Furthermore, even the lame, the blind, the dead, the mute, and those with infantile paralysis can be made whole. Their eyes come to see, and they come to walk, and even the dead are raised.

The enemy devil will fear and tremble, so those who are captured by demons or power of darkness will be freed (Mark 16:17-18). There will be manifestations of healing works going beyond the limitations of time and space. Extraordinary works can also happen through the things that we possess such as handkerchiefs as in the case of Paul (Acts 19:11-12).

Also, just as Jesus calmed down wind and waves, we will be able to cause a change in the weather conditions (Matthew 8:26-27). Rains will stop, and we can even change the course of a typhoon or a hurricane or make it disappear. We can even see rainbows on a very clear day.

Other than these, if we are called sons of God, we will enter into New Jerusalem which houses God's throne. There we can enjoy the honor and glory as true children. If we have faith to be saved, we will enter into Paradise, but if we become true children who are called sons of God, we can enter into New Jerusalem, the most beautiful dwelling place of the heavenly kingdom.

How great is the honor and glory of a prince who will receive the throne? And if we resemble God who is the Ruler of everything and are called sons of God, our honor and dignity will be very great! We will be escorted by the heavenly host and angels, and we will be praised by countless people in the heavenly kingdom forever.

Moreover, we will enjoy all kinds of beautiful things and grand and magnificent houses in splendid New Jerusalem. We will live forever in an inexpressible magnitude of happiness.

Therefore, we should take up our own cross and become peacemakers with the heart of the Lord who has sacrificed Himself to the point of being crucified, so that we can receive God's great love and blessings.

Chapter 8
The Eighth Blessing

Blessed Are Those Who Have Been Persecuted
for the Sake of Righteousness,
for Theirs Is the Kingdom of Heaven

Matthew 5:10

Blessed are those who have been persecuted for the sake of righteousness, for theirs is the kingdom of heaven.

"Believe in Jesus Christ and receive salvation."

"You can receive blessings in all things by believing in the almighty God."

Often preachers say that when we believe in Jesus Christ, we can receive salvation and blessings in all things, and we can be prosperous in our lives receiving answers to all kinds of life's problems.

In our church alone we give glory to God with so many testimonies every week.

However, the Bible also tells us that there will be hardships and persecutions when we believe in Jesus Christ. We will receive blessings of eternal life and blessings on this earth to the extent that we give up and sacrifice for the Lord's sake, but then we will also receive persecutions as well (Philippians 1:29).

> *Truly I say to you, there is no one who has left house or brothers or sisters or mother or father or children or farms, for My sake and for the gospel's sake, but that he will receive a hundred times as much now in the present age, houses and brothers and sisters and mothers and children and farms, along with persecutions; and in the age to come, eternal life (Mark 10:29-30).*

Being Persecuted for Righteousness

What does it mean to be persecuted for righteousness? It is the persecution that we face when we live by the word of God following truth, goodness, and light.

Of course, we don't have to face persecutions if we just compromise and do not lead a proper Christian life. But 2 Timothy 3:12 says, *"Indeed, all who desire to live godly in Christ Jesus will be persecuted."* If we follow the word of God, we may face difficulties or receive persecutions for no reason.

For example, when we did not believe in the Lord, we could have been drinking and using offensive language and showing rough behavior. But after receiving grace from God, we try to quit drinking and live a godly life. So, we will naturally be inclined to distance ourselves from unbelieving colleagues and associates. Even if we do associate with them, they cannot enjoy the same things with us like before, so they may be disappointed or say something against our new behavior.

In my case too, before I accepted the Lord, I had many friends who drank with me. Also, when relatives gathered we would drink a lot. But after I accepted the Lord, I understood, in a revival meeting, the will of God in telling us not to be drunk, and I quit drinking immediately.

I did not serve any alcoholic drinks to my brothers, other relatives or friends. So they were complaining to me that I was not treating them as I was supposed to treat them.

Furthermore, after we accept the Lord and to keep the

Lord's Day holy, we sometimes cannot attend some outings held by our workplace or other social meetings. In a family which is not evangelized we may even face persecutions because we wouldn't bow before idols.

The Evil Hate Light

Then, why should we suffer when we believe in the Lord? This is the same as oil and water do not mix. God is Light, and those who believe in the Lord and live in the word spiritually belong to Light (1 John 1:5). But the master of this world is the enemy devil and Satan, the ruler of darkness (Ephesians 6:12).

Therefore, just as the darkness disappears where there is light, when the number of believers who are like the light increases, the ruling power of the enemy devil and Satan will decrease. The enemy devil and Satan control the worldly people who belong to them. They incite them to persecute believers so that they will not be believers any more.

John 3:20-21 says, *"For everyone who does evil hates the Light, and does not come to the Light for fear that his deeds will be exposed. But he who practices the truth comes to the Light, so that his deeds may be manifested as having been wrought in God."*

Those who have good hearts may be touched and accept the gospel when they see others living by the word of God in righteousness. But those who are evil will think of such a thing as being foolish. They hate it and persecute the believers for it.

Some try to persuade the believers with their logic. They say, "Do you have to be such an extremist? There are people who are raised in Christian families. Some of them are elders in a church, but they still drink." But God's children should never act in the unrighteousness that God hates just because their colleagues, relatives, or friends have their feelings hurt a little bit momentarily.

God gave His one and only Son for us who were sinners. Jesus took all kinds of mockeries and persecutions, and finally died on the cross taking our sins. If we think of this love, we cannot compromise with the world under any kind of persecution just for momentary comfort.

Cases of Being Persecuted for Righteousness

In 605 BC, by the invasion of Nebuchadnezzar of Babylon, Shadrach, Meshach, and Abednego became captives along with Daniel. Even in foreign culture that was lustful and full of idolatry, they kept their reverence and faith in God.

One day, they faced a very difficult situation. The king made a golden statue and made every person in the country bow down before it. If anybody disobeyed the king's order, he would be thrown into fiery furnace.

Shadrach, Meshach, and Abednego could have easily avoided any trouble just by bowing down once, but they never bowed down.

It's because Exodus 20:4-5 says, *"You shall not make for yourself an idol, or any likeness of what is in heaven above or on the earth beneath or in the water under the earth. You shall not worship them or serve them; for I, the LORD your God, am a jealous God, visiting the iniquity of the fathers on the children, on the third and the fourth generations of those who hate Me."*

Finally, Daniel's three friends had to be thrown into fiery furnace. How touching their confession was at this moment!

> *If it be so, our God whom we serve is able to deliver us from the furnace of blazing fire; and He will deliver us out of your hand, O king. But even if He does not, let it be known to you, O king, that we are not going to serve your gods or worship the golden image that you have set up (Daniel 3:17-18).*

Even in a life-threatening situation, they did not compromise to keep their faith. God saw their faith and saved them from the fiery furnace.

Being Persecuted Due to One's Own Shortcomings

One thing we have to remember here is that there are

many cases where they are persecuted because of their own shortcomings rather being persecuted for righteousness like Daniel's three friends.

For example, there are some believers who do not fulfill all their duties saying that they are doing God's works.

If students do not study and if the housewives do not take care of housekeeping to concentrate on church activities, they will be persecuted from their family members. The cause of the persecution is that they neglect their studies or housekeeping work. But they misunderstand that they are being persecuted because they are doing the Lord's work.

A believer may not be very hard working in his workplace, and he tries to shift his own work on to another person giving excuses of church works. Then, he will be warned or rebuked in his workplace. This is not being persecuted for righteousness.

So 1 Peter 2:19-20 says, *"For this finds favor, if for the sake of conscience toward God a person bears up under sorrows when suffering unjustly. For what credit is there if, when you sin and are harshly treated, you endure it with patience? But if when you do what is right and suffer for it you patiently endure it, this finds favor with God."*

Blessed Are Those Who Are Persecuted for Righteousness' Sake

Matthew 5:10 says, *"Blessed are those who have been*

persecuted for the sake of righteousness, for theirs is the kingdom of heaven." Why does the Bible say they are blessed? The persecutions one receives because of evil or lawlessness cannot be blessings or rewards. But the persecution for the sake of righteousness is a blessing because he who receives such persecution can possess the heavenly kingdom.

As the ground becomes harder after rain, after going through persecutions, our heart will be firmer and more perfect. We can find the untruths of which we were unaware before and cast them off. We can cultivate meekness and peace and resemble the heart of the Lord to love even our enemies.

Before, if we were struck on one cheek we would get angry and we would have to hit back. But through persecutions, we come to learn about service and love so that we can now even turn the other cheek.

Also, those who used to become sad and complain when faced with difficulties can have firm faith through persecutions. They now have hope for the heavenly kingdom and they are thankful and joyful in any kind of situation.

Let me tell you a real-life example. One of our church members had troubles with his colleague in his office over just about every matter. That person would slander the believer for no reason. His actions lacked common sensibility, and this believer had to suffer a lot because of it.

Other people used to say that he was a nice man, but through this situation the believer found out that he also had hatred in his heart. He made up his mind to embrace his colleague in his heart for God tells us to love even our enemies. He remembered what this person liked and occasionally gave some to him.

Also, as he prayed for this person, he gained true love for him, and their relationship became closer and friendlier than that of any of the other office workers.

So, Psalm 119:71 says, *"It is good for me that I was afflicted, that I may learn Your statutes."* Through such suffering we come to humble ourselves more. We cast off sins and evil relying on the Lord and become sanctified. In time the persecutions will naturally disappear.

If we are persecuted for righteousness, our faith will grow up. Then, we will be respected by others around us and also receive spiritual and material blessings that God is giving to us. Furthermore, to the extent that we accomplish righteousness in us, we can advance into better places in the heavenly kingdom. So just how great a blessing this is!

Heavenly Dwelling Places and Glories are Different

Then, what is the difference between the heaven that those who are poor in heart possess and the heaven that those who are persecuted for righteousness possess? In fact there is a great difference.

The former is the heaven with a general meaning into

which everyone who is saved can go. But the latter means that we will go into better dwelling places in heaven to the extent that we are persecuted for acting in righteousness.

To the extent that we accomplish sanctification and become true children that God wants, and according to how well we fulfill our duties, the dwelling places and the rewards in heaven will be different.

John 14:2 says, *"In My Father's house are many dwelling places; if it were not so, I would have told you; for I go to prepare a place for you."*

Also, 1 Corinthians 15:41 says, *"There is one glory of the sun, and another glory of the moon, and another glory of the stars; for star differs from star in glory."* We can see that the dwelling places and the glory we will have in heaven will be different according to what extent of righteousness we achieve.

The poor in heart are the ones who have accepted the Lord and have gained the right to enter into the heavenly kingdom. From then on, they can become the meek and have pure hearts by mourning and repenting of their sins to cast them off. They have to keep on growing in their faith by following righteousness continually.

Namely only those who realize their evilness, cast it off and become sanctified through persecutions and trials can enter into better places in heaven and also see God the Father.

Persecutions for the Lord

To the extent that we accomplish righteousness, the persecutions will disappear. As our faith grows and we become more and more perfect, we will be respected by people around us. Furthermore, we can also receive spiritual and material blessings from God.

We can see this in the case of the three friends of Daniel. They were persecuted because they held on to their righteousness for God. They were thrown into the fiery furnace that was seven times hotter than before, but God protected them. Not one hair on their head was singed.

Seeing this work of God, the king also gave glory to God the Almighty. He also lifted up these three.

But it doesn't mean that all persecutions will go away just because we have accomplished righteousness completely by practicing the word of God. There are also persecutions that the Lord's workers have to go through for the kingdom of God.

> *Blessed are you when people insult you and persecute you, and falsely say all kinds of evil against you because of Me. Rejoice and be glad, for your reward in heaven is great; for in the same way they persecuted the prophets who were before you (Matthew 5:11-12).*

Many fathers of faith willingly took up sufferings to fulfill the will of God. First of all, Jesus existed in the form of God. He is blameless and spotless, but He took the punishment of sinners. In order to fulfill the providence of salvation, He was flogged and was crucified in the midst of all kinds of mockeries and contempt.

The Apostle Paul

Let's consider the case of the apostle Paul. Paul laid the foundation of world mission by preaching the gospel to the Gentiles. Through his three mission journeys he established many churches. This was by no means easy. We can see how difficult it was in his confession.

> *Are they servants of Christ? I speak as if insane I more so; in far more labors, in far more imprisonments, beaten times without number, often in danger of death. Five times I received from the Jews thirty-nine lashes. Three times I was beaten with rods, once I was stoned, three times I was shipwrecked, a night and a day I have spent in the deep. I have been in labor and hardship, through many sleepless nights, in hunger and thirst, often without food, in cold and exposure (2 Corinthians 11:23-27).*

There were even people who vowed not to eat anything until they killed Paul. We can imagine how great the suffering was that he went through (Acts 23:12). But no matter what the situation of the persecutions, the apostle Paul was always joyful and thankful because he had hope for the heavenly kingdom.

He was faithful to the point of death for the kingdom and righteousness of God, not even sparing his own life (2 Timothy 4:7-8).

It's not that men of God are suffering because they don't have the power. When Jesus was on the cross, if He had only wanted, He could have called more than 12 legions of angels and destroyed all the evil ones there (Matthew 26:53).

Both Moses and the apostle Paul had such great power that people even considered them as gods (Exodus 7:1, Acts 14:8-11). When people took handkerchiefs or aprons that had touched Paul to the sick, the diseases left them and demons were driven out from them (Acts 19:12).

But because they knew that God's providence would be fulfilled more greatly through their sufferings, they did not try to avoid or get away from sufferings but took them with joy. They preached the will of God with burning passion and did what God had commanded them to do.

Great Reward When We Rejoice and Are Glad

The reason why we can rejoice and be glad when we are persecuted for the name of the Lord is because great will be the reward in the heavenly kingdom (Matthew 5:11-12).

Among the loyal ministers in old days, there were some who were willing to sacrifice their lives for the king. The king would add more glory and honor for their loyalty. If the minister had died, the king would give rewards to his children.

As said in John 15:13, *"Greater love has no one than this, that one lay down his life for his friends,"* they proved their love for their king by sacrificing their lives.

If we are persecuted and even give up our lives for the Lord, how can God, being the Master of all things, just let the matter remain as it is? He will pour down on us with unimaginable heavenly blessings.

He will give us better dwelling places in the heavenly kingdom. Those who are martyred for the Lord will be acknowledged for their heart that loves the Lord. They will go into at least the third kingdom of heaven or even New Jerusalem.

Even if we are not fully sanctified, if we can sacrifice our lives to become martyrs, it means that we can become completely sanctified if more time is given.

The apostle Paul suffered so much and even gave his life for the Lord. He could communicate with God clearly and experience many spiritual things of heaven. Since he had seen Paradise, he confessed, *"For I consider that the sufferings of this present time are not worthy to be compared with the glory that is to be revealed to us"* (Romans 8:18).

He also confessed in 2 Timothy 4:7-8, *"I have fought the good fight, I have finished the course, I have kept the faith; in the future there is laid up for me the crown of righteousness, which the Lord, the righteous Judge, will award to me on that day."*

God does not forget the faithfulness and effort of those who are persecuted and even become martyrs for the Lord. He pays back such sacrifice with overflowing honor and rewards. As the apostle Paul confessed, there will be amazing rewards and glory that await.

Even if we do not actually lose our physical life, all the things that we do for the Lord with heart of martyrdom and all the persecutions that we go through for the Lord will be paid back as rewards and blessings.

Also, to those who rejoice and are glad even though they are persecuted for the Lord, God answers to their heart's desires and fills their needs to show the evidence that God is with them. To the extent that they overcome hardships, their faith will be greater; then they will receive greater power and authority, communicate with God more clearly and be able to manifest greater works of God's power.

But in fact, for those who sacrifice their lives for the Lord do not care if they don't receive anything back on this earth. They can rejoice even more because nothing can be compared with the heavenly blessings and rewards that they will receive later.

Blessings for Those Who Participate in the Sufferings of the Lord

We should remember one more thing. When a man of God suffers for the Lord, those who are with him will also receive blessings.

When David was being chased as a result of his sin by his son Absalom, those who were truthful knew that David was a man of God. Even if their lives were threatened they still stayed with him. Finally, when David received God's grace again, they could receive the grace together with him.

This is the will of the just God that when a man of God suffers for the name of the Lord, those who are with him with truthful hearts will also participate in his glory later. Jesus also told His disciples about the heavenly rewards they would receive to give them more hope.

> *You are those who have stood by Me in My trials; and just as My Father has granted Me a kingdom, I grant you that you may eat and drink at My table in My kingdom, and you will sit on thrones judging the twelve tribes of Israel (Luke 22:28-30).*

Our church and I had to go through many persecutions in accomplishing God's kingdom. Because we knew it was the will of God, we preached about deep spiritual things, knowing that it would also cause persecutions for us.

Going through many difficulties that a man cannot really bear with, we left everything into God's hands with only prayers and fasting. Then, God gave us greater power as evidence that He is with us. He let us manifest so many signs and wonders. Not only numerous diseases were healed but also the infirmities such as infantile paralysis, blindness and deafness, or parts of the body that had been weak since birth were made well.

Furthermore, we could lead hundreds of thousands and even millions of people to the side of the Lord through crusades in many countries. One of those crusades caught the attention of the whole world as it was reported by CNN (Cable News Network).

In 2005, GCN (Global Christian Network) TV was established and it began airing 24-hour-a-day broadcasting in New York City and New Jersey. In just 1 year since the establishment, God blessed it in a way that anybody can watch it anywhere in the world through satellite.

Especially, in the New York Crusade in July 2006 held at Madison Square Garden in New York City, the crusade was broadcast to more than 200 countries around the globe through various Christian broadcasters such as GCN, Cosmovision, GloryStar Network, and Daystar TV.

Behind this kind of glory were the tearful prayers of the church members. Most church members kept the church with prayers and fasting when the church was in a difficult situation.

Those who participated in the suffering with the Lord had overflowing hope for the heavenly kingdom. They grew up to have bold and spiritual faith. All these things were given back to them as blessings. Their families, workplaces, and businesses were blessed. They give glory to God with their many testimonies.

Therefore, those who follow true blessing are able to rejoice and be glad from the bottom of their hearts when they are persecuted for the Lord. It's because they will look forward to the eternal blessings that they will receive in the heavenly kingdom.

One Who Pursues True Blessing

A blessing in the sight of God is very different from the blessings that the worldly people think of to be blessings.

Most people think being rich is blessing. But, God says the poor in heart are blessed. People think just being always happy is blessing. But, God says those who mourn are blessed. God says those who are hungry and thirsty for righteousness and who are meek are blessed.

The Beatitudes contain the blessed and true ways to possess

the kingdom of heaven with heart that is poor and to resemble the heart of God through persecutions.

Thus, if we just obey the word, we will be able to cast off all forms of evil and fill our hearts with truth. We will be able to completely recover the meek and holy image of God and be pleasing to God. This is the way to become a man of faith and a man of whole spirit.

This kind of person is like a tree planted by water. Trees planted by water are supplied with fresh water in abundance. Even in drought or hot days, they will have green leaves and bear abundant fruit (Jeremiah 17:7-8).

The believers who are living in the word of God from whom all blessings flow, will have nothing to fear even in difficulties. They will always experience the hands of God's love and blessings.

Therefore, I pray in the name of the Lord that you will look forward to the glory that will be revealed to you and cultivate the Beatitudes in you. I pray that you will be able to enjoy true blessings that God the Father is giving to you to the fullest degree, both on this earth and in heaven.

*"How blessed is the man
who does not walk
in the counsel of the wicked,
Nor stand in the path of sinners,
Nor sit in the seat of scoffers!
But his delight is in the law of the LORD,
And in His law he meditates day and night.*

*He will be like a tree firmly planted
by streams of water,
Which yields its fruit in its season
And its leaf does not wither;
And in whatever he does,
he prospers"
(Psalm 1:1-3).*

The Author
Dr. Jaerock Lee

Dr. Jaerock Lee was born in Muan, Jeonnam Province, Republic of Korea, in 1943. In his twenties, he suffered from a variety of incurable diseases for seven years and awaited death with no hope for recovery. One day in the spring of 1974, however, he was led to a church by his sister, and when he knelt down to pray, the living God immediately healed him of all his diseases.

From the moment Dr. Lee met the living God through that wonderful experience, he has loved God with all his heart and sincerity, and in 1978 was called to be a servant of God. He prayed fervently so that he could clearly understand the will of God and wholly accomplish it, and obeyed all the word of God. In 1982, he founded Manmin Church in Seoul, S. Korea, and countless works of God, including miraculous healings and wonders, have been taking place at his church.

In 1986, Dr. Lee was ordained as a pastor at the Annual Assembly of Jesus' Sungkyul Church of Korea, and four years later in 1990, his sermons began to be broadcast on the Far East Broadcasting Company, the Asia Broadcast Station, and the Washington Christian Radio System to Australia, Russia, the Philippines, and many more.

Three years later in 1993, Manmin Central Church was selected as one of the "World's Top 50 Churches" by the *Christian World* magazine (US) and he received an Honorary Doctorate of Divinity from Christian Faith College, Florida, USA, and in 1996 a Ph. D. in Ministry from Kingsway Theological Seminary, Iowa, USA.

Since 1993, Dr. Lee has taken the lead in world mission through many overseas crusades in L.A., New York, Baltimore, Hawaii of the USA, Tanzania, Argentina, Uganda, Japan, Pakistan, Kenya, the Philippines,

Honduras, India, Russia, Germany, Peru, and Democratic Republic of Congo, and in 2002 he was called a "worldwide pastor" by major Christian newspapers in Korea for his work in various overseas crusades.

As of August 2009, Manmin Central Church is a congregation of more than 100,000 members and has 9,000 branch churches throughout the globe including 52 domestic branch churches in major cities, and has so far commissioned more than 133 missionaries to 25 countries, including the United States, Russia, Germany, Canada, Japan, China, France, India, Kenya, and many more.

To this day, Dr. Lee has written 57 books, including bestsellers *Tasting Eternal Life before Death*, *My Life My Faith I & II*, *The Way of Salvation*, *The Measure of Faith*, *Heaven I & II*, and *Hell*, and his works have been being translated into more than 41 languages.

His Christian columns appear on *The Hankook Ilbo, The JoongAng Daily, The Dong-A Ilbo, The Munhwa Ilbo, The Seoul Shinmun, The Kyunghyang Shinmun, The Hankyoreh Shinmun, The Korea Economic Daily, The Korea Herald, The Shisa News, The Christian Press* and *The Nation Evangelization Newspaper*.

Dr. Lee is currently leader of many missionary organizations and associations including: Chairman, The United Holiness Church of Jesus Christ; Permanent President of the World Christianity Revival Mission Association; President, The Nation Evangelization Newspaper; President, Manmin World Mission; Founder, Manmin TV; Founder & Board Chairman, Global Christian Network (GCN); Founder & Board Chairman, World Christian Doctors Network (WCDN); and Founder & Board Chairman, Manmin International Seminary (MIS).

Other powerful books by the same author

Heaven I & II

A detailed sketch of the gorgeous living environment the heavenly citizens enjoy and beautiful description of different levels of heavenly kingdoms.

The Message of the Cross

A powerful awakening message for all the people who are spiritually asleep In this book you will find the reason Jesus is the only Savior and the true love of God.

Hell

An earnest message to all mankind from God, who wishes not even one soul to fall into the depths of hell! You will discover the never-before-revealed account of the cruel reality of the Lower Grave and hell.

Tasting Eternal Life Before Death

A testimonial memoirs of Dr. Jaerock Lee, who was born gain and saved from the valley of death and has been leading an exemplary Christian life.

The Measure of Faith

What kind of a dwelling place, crown and reward are prepared for you in heaven? This book provides with wisdom and guidance for you to measure your faith and cultivate the best and most mature faith.

www.urimbooks.com

www.ingramcontent.com/pod-product-compliance
Lightning Source LLC
LaVergne TN
LVHW010329070526
838199LV00065B/5703